MW00608373

COUNSELING ON THE WALL!

Easy-To-Make Bulletin Boards To Reinforce Your Valuable Guidance/Classroom Lessons

By Rosanne Sheritz Sartori

Dedication

This book is dedicated to Arden Martenz, publisher of Mar*co Products. I can't thank her enough for giving me the opportunity to be an author. Arden recognized that my ideas might be useful to other counselors looking for ways to reach and teach children. What's more, she's always willing and ready to take on another big project! She deserves an award for the impact she's made in the field of school counseling. But since neither Oscars nor Emmys are awarded in our field, she might have to settle for my thanks.

I also want to thank my husband Glenn. He's a wonderful sounding board and editor who should be given an honorary degree in counseling. He has heard it all and always gives me an honest opinion.

Counseling On The Wall!

Easy-To-Make Bulletin Boards To Reinforce Your Valuable Guidance/Classroom Lessons

10-DIGIT ISBN: 1-57543-171-8
13-DIGIT ISBN: 978-1-57543-171-0

COPYRIGHT © 2009 MAR*CO PRODUCTS, INC

Published by Mar*co Products, Inc.
1443 Old York Road
Warminster, PA 18974
1-800-448-2197
www.marcoproducts.com

Graphic Design: Cameon Funk

Clipart from: www.graphicsfactory.com and www.clipart.com

PERMISSION TO REPRODUCE: The purchaser may reproduce the activity sheets, free and without special permission, for participant use for a particular group or class. Reproduction of these materials for an entire school system is forbidden.

All rights reserved. Except as provided above, no part of this book may be reproduced or transmitted in whole or in part in any form or by any means, electronic or mechanical, including photocopying, recording, or by any information storage or retrieval system without permission in writing by the publisher.

PRINTED IN THE U.S.A.

Table Of Contents

Introduction

Being an elementary counselor is a demanding job. Classroom guidance lessons, small groups, individual counseling, meetings, and conferences make counselors wish we had super powers. And on top of all our other job demands, that blank bulletin board is awaiting transformation into a work of art.

Counseling On The Wall! has come to your rescue! In this book, you'll find easy-to-implement ideas to dress up a blank bulletin board—whether you only have a few minutes to post a few meaningful quotations or time to create a showy display. The quotes used in this book are credited to the famous people whose words have inspired all of us. Those without a credit were written by someone who worked as an educator for 30 years—ME!

Each bulletin board's reproducible components are provided in PDF format on the included CD (see inside back cover). Simply print and, if necessary, cut out/apart the required pieces. Each bulletin board's PDF file folder also contains a sample color board. Based on a 5' x 4' bulletin board, these designs can be modified to accommodate smaller or larger boards. Background colors, borders, and layout are only suggestions. Mix the components from different samples to create unique, meaningful boards.

Maybe you're getting ready for a school open house or parent-teacher conferences and you'd like to create an eye-catching display. Showcasing every child's work can be time-consuming, but quite impressive. Don't be confined by the bulletin board's borders. Extend your display to the wall surrounding the board.

Bulletin board ideas and mini-posters are divided into 14 units spanning the National Standards, which the American School Counselor Association believes to be the essential elements of a quality and effective school-counseling program. Creating these bulletin boards will reinforce your school's guidance program and help assure your compliance with the ASCA National Standards.

Rosanne Sheritz Sartori

Getting Started

Unless your boards are nicely covered, start by creating an attractive background. We've suggested colored mural paper, but wrapping paper, wallpaper, or fabric also work well.

Borders add interest. Create your own, use some of the many borders in *Counseling On The Wall!*, or buy ready-to-use borders from a classroom/teacher-supply store. If you use this book's printable PDF borders, frame the board with multiple copies.

Most *Counseling On The Wall!* bulletin boards include a message or unifying title in printable PDF format. If you choose not to use the PDF title, you may spell out the message with letters purchased from a classroom/teacher-supply store.

The ideas in this book can be adapted to suit your needs. Mix, match, and implement them to jump start your displays. *Counseling On The Wall!* will get you started. The rest is up to you and your imagination. The possibilities are limitless.

Classroom guidance lessons, small-group and individual counseling, meetings, conferences—*and* beautiful, meaningful bulletin boards ... maybe you *do* have super powers, after all!

COUNSELING ON THE WALL! © 2009 MAR✶CO PRODUCTS, INC. 1-800-448-2197

Instructions For Using The CD

The CD found on the inside back cover provides ADOBE® PDF files of each bulletin boards reproducible components.

We recommend that you print these components on medium-weight copy paper. Some of the pages require cutting/gluing.

These files cannot be modified/edited.

System requirements to open PDF (.pdf) files:

Adobe Reader® 5.0 or newer (compatible with Windows 2000® or newer or Mac OS 9.0® or newer).

This CD may not be duplicated or distributed.

PERMISSION TO REPRODUCE: The purchaser may reproduce the bulletin board patterns/templates, free and without special permission, for participant use for a particular group or class. Sharing these files with other counselors/faculty members or reproduction of these materials for an entire school system is forbidden.

COUNSELING ON THE WALL! © 2009 MAR✳CO PRODUCTS, INC. 1-800-448-2197

UNIT 1

Self

Most elementary counselors work hard to encourage students to believe in themselves. The term *self-esteem* has fallen out of favor in recent years because critics believe that children brimming with self-confidence will be selfish and self-centered.

Elementary counselors know that their purpose is not to create children who shout, "Me, Me, ME!" The counselor simply tries to assure every student that he/she is a special, unique person who has the same rights and responsibilities as everyone else.

This section's boards can help you accomplish this goal.

ASCA STANDARDS
FOR UNIT 1—SELF

PERSONAL/SOCIAL DEVELOPMENT	
Standard A: Students will acquire the knowledge, attitudes and interpersonal skills to help them understand and respect self and others.	
PS:A1	**Acquire Self-Knowledge**
PS:A1.1	Develop positive attitudes toward self as a unique and worthy person
PS:A1.10	Identify personal strengths and assets
PS:A2	**Acquire Interpersonal Skills**
PS:A2.2	Respect alternative points of view
PS:A2.3	Recognize, accept, respect and appreciate individual differences

COUNSELING ON THE WALL! © 2009 MAR✳CO PRODUCTS, INC. 1-800-448-2197

THERE IS NO ONE QUITE LIKE ME!

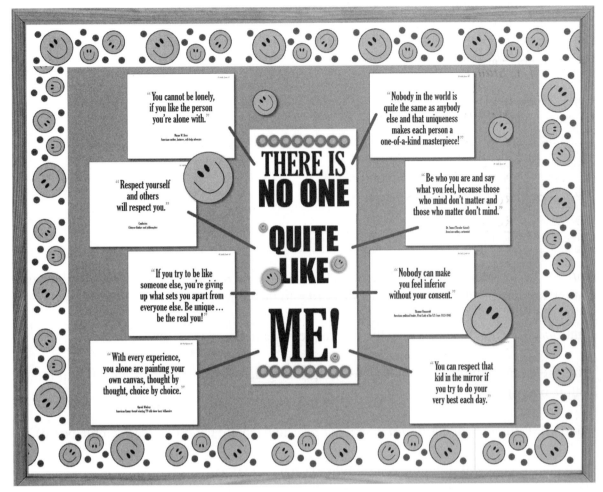

SAMPLE BOARD IS BASED ON A 5' WIDE X 4' TALL BULLETIN BOARD

Objective: To help the student develop positive attitudes toward him/herself as a unique and worthy person

Time: One 30-40 minute class period

Materials Needed:

For the leader:
- ☐ Blue mural paper for the bulletin board background
- ☐ *Optional: Board 1 Smiley Face Border* cut in half (included on CD)
- ☐ *Board 1 Title* (included on CD) or make the title from purchased bulletin board letters

11

- ☐ Selected *Board 1 Quotations About Self* (included on CD)
- ☐ *Optional: Board 1 Smiley Faces* cut out (included on CD)
- ☐ White and/or colored paper for printing copies, preferably medium-weight
- ☐ Stapler and staples or glue
- ☐ Scissors
- ☐ *Optional:* Yarn

For each student:
- ☐ Scrap paper
- ☐ Pencil

Pre-Presentation Preparation:

Cover the bulletin board with blue mural paper.

Optional: Print enough copies of the *Board 1 Smiley Face Border* to frame the bulletin board. Cut the borders in half. Staple or glue the border to the bulletin board (see sample board).

Print *Board 1 Title*. Staple or glue the title to the bulletin board (see sample board).

Print the desired number of quotations. Staple or glue the quotations around the title (see sample board).

Optional: Print and cut out *Board 1 Smiley Faces* to decorate the board (see sample board).

Optional: Stretch yarn from the central title to each quotation.

Directions:

Explain that this lesson centers around the sayings on the bulletin board and will help students understand themselves.

Ask several students to explain what the bulletin board title means to them.

After reading each quotation aloud, ask how it relates to what a person thinks about him/herself.

Number each quotation. Each student selects the quotation that he/she feels best explains the bulletin board title and writes its number on the scrap paper. Tally the collected papers. Announce which quotation was chosen most often.

COUNSELING ON THE WALL! © 2009 MAR★CO PRODUCTS, INC. 1-800-448-2197

WE'RE PROUD OF OUR CLASSROOMS

SAMPLE BOARD IS BASED ON A 5' WIDE X 4' TALL BULLETIN BOARD

Objective: To teach students to recognize, accept, respect, and appreciate individual differences

Time: One 30-40 minute class period for each participating classroom

Materials Needed:

For the leader:

☐ Blue mural paper for the bulletin board background

☐ *Optional: Board 2 Star Border* cut in half (included on CD)

☐ *Board 2 Title* (included on CD) or make the title from purchased bulletin board letters

☐ *Optional: Board 2 Star Patterns* cut out (included on CD)
☐ White and/or colored paper for printing copies, preferably medium-weight
☐ Stapler and staples or glue
☐ Scissors

For each classroom in the school:
☐ *Board 2 Classroom Bar Graph* (included on CD)
☐ Markers or colored pencils to make the bar graphs colorful

Pre-Presentation Preparation:

Cover the bulletin board with blue mural paper.

Optional: Print enough copies of the *Board 2 Star Border* to frame the bulletin board. Cut the borders in half. Staple or glue the border to the bulletin board (see sample board).

Print *Board 2 Title*. Staple or glue the title to the bulletin board (see sample board).

Print one blank *Board 2 Classroom Bar Graph* for each classroom in the school

Optional: Print copies of the *Board 2 Star Patterns*. Cut out the stars to decorate the board (see sample board).

Directions:

Tell the students you'd like to get to know them better and to share what you learn about them on a bulletin board. Explain that other classrooms will also be represented on the bulletin board, so students will be able to get to know about students other than their classmates. Ask if the students are familiar with bar graphs.

As you complete the *Classroom Bar Graph*, demonstrate why a graph is a good way to display information. Or have a student fill in the graph as you obtain the:

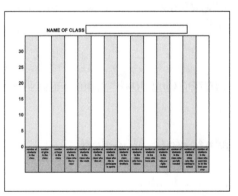

- • number of students in the class
- • number of girls in the class
- • number of boys in the class
- • number of students in the class who like to read
- • number of students in the class who like math
- • number of students in the class who like art
- • number of students in the class who like to participate in sports
- • number of students in the class who have at least one brother

COUNSELING ON THE WALL! © 2009 MAR✶CO PRODUCTS, INC. 1-800-448-2197

- number of students in the class who have at least one sister
- number of students in the class who have at least one pet
- number of students in the class who are right-handed
- number of students in the class who are left-handed
- number of students in the class who like coming to school
- number of students in the class who want this to be the best year ever

Staple or glue the graphs around the title, then staple or glue the stars next to the graphs.

Students orally summarize similarities and differences between classroom graphs. For example: Miss Jones' first-grade class and Miss Smith's first-grade class have the same number of boys and girls. Miss Smith's room has more students who prefer reading to math. Miss Jones' class has more students who prefer math to reading.

COUNSELING ON THE WALL! © 2009 MAR✲CO PRODUCTS, INC. 1-800-448-2197

I AM ME...A GOOD WAY TO BE!

SAMPLE BOARD IS BASED ON A 5' WIDE X 4' TALL BULLETIN BOARD

Objective: To help the student develop positive attitudes toward him/herself as a unique and worthy person and learn to identify personal strengths and assets

(*Note:* This bulletin board uses glyphs. A *glyph* is a symbol that conveys information without words. This project provides a fun way for students to share information about themselves and reinforces the idea that each person is special and unique. It's a great accompaniment to a guidance lesson about being special and unique.)

Time: One 40-60 minute class period

Materials Needed:

For the leader:
- ☐ Red mural paper for the bulletin board background
- ☐ *Optional: Board 3 Crayon Border* cut in half (included on CD)
- ☐ *Board 3 Title* (included on CD) or make the title from purchased bulletin board letters
- ☐ *Optional: Board 3 Star Patterns* cut out (included on CD)
- ☐ *Board 3 Glyph Key* (included on CD)
- ☐ White and/or colored paper for printing copies, preferably medium-weight
- ☐ Scissors
- ☐ Stapler and staples or glue

For each student:
- ☐ *Board 3 Paper Doll Glyph Shape* (included on CD)
- ☐ Crayons, markers, or colored pencils

Pre-Presentation Preparation:

Cover the bulletin board with red mural paper.

Optional: Print enough copies of the *Board 3 Crayon Border* to frame the bulletin board. Cut the borders in half. Staple or glue the border to the bulletin board (see sample board).

Print *Board 3 Title*. Staple or glue the title to the bulletin board (see sample board).

Print and cut apart *Board 3 Paper Doll Glyph Shapes*.

Print the *Board 3 Glyph Key*.

Optional: Print copies of the *Board 3 Star Patterns*. Cut out the stars to decorate the board (see sample board).

Directions:

Tell the students you're going to put up a bulletin board that will show how special they are.

Each student writes his/her name in the rectangle above the *Paper Doll Glyph Shape*. Using the *Glyph Key*, read the number and directions aloud. Give the students time to follow the directions.

COUNSELING ON THE WALL! © 2009 MAR✴CO PRODUCTS, INC. 1-800-448-2197

Glyph Key:

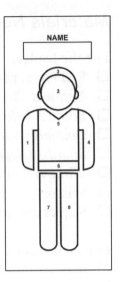

1. Color the left arm pink if you're a girl.
   Color the left arm blue if you're a boy.

2. Draw a face using the number 2 as the nose.

3. Color the hair purple if you have a sister or sisters.
   Color the hair orange if you have a brother or brothers.
   Color the hair green if you have at least one brother and at least one sister.

4. Color the right arm yellow if you like reading better than math.
   Color the right arm red if you like math better than reading.

5. Color the body blue if your birthday is in January, February, or March.
   Color the body green if your birthday is in April, May, or June.
   Color the body orange if your birthday is July, August, or September.
   Color the body yellow if your birthday is in October, November, or December.

6. Color the belt black if you like cookies better than ice cream.
   Color the belt brown if you like ice cream better than cookies.

7. Color the left leg orange if you like sports better than art.
   Color the left leg green if you like art better than sports.

8. Color the right leg purple if you have a pet.
   Color the right leg yellow if you do not have a pet.

Staple or glue the completed glyphs around the bulletin board title.

Post the *Glyph Key* on the board so everyone can interpret the drawings.

Ask if the students can find two identical glyphs. If they find two exactly alike, ask:

Does that mean these two people are exactly the same? (No. They might have several things in common, but everyone is unique.)

COUNSELING ON THE WALL! © 2009 MAR✳CO PRODUCTS, INC. 1-800-448-2197

YOU ARE A MASTERPIECE!

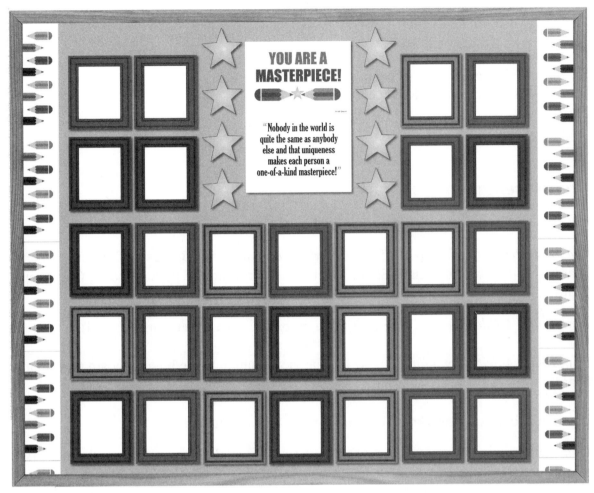

SAMPLE BOARD IS BASED ON A 5′ WIDE X 4′ TALL BULLETIN BOARD

Objective: To help students develop positive attitudes and accept, respect, and appreciate individual differences

Time: One 40–60 minute class period

Materials Needed:

For the leader:
- ☐ Yellow or gold mural paper for the bulletin board background
- ☐ *Optional: Board 4 Colored Pencil Border* cut in half (included on CD)
- ☐ *Board 4 Title* (included on CD) or make the title from purchased bulletin board letters
- ☐ *Board 4 Self Quotation 6* (included on CD)

☐ *Optional: Board 4 Star Patterns* cut out (included on CD)
☐ Scissors
☐ White and/or colored paper for printing copies, preferably medium-weight
☐ Stapler and staples or glue

For each student:
☐ *Board 4 Picture Frame* (included on CD)
☐ Crayons, markers, or colored pencils
☐ Scissors
☐ *Optional:* Mirrors

Pre-Presentation Preparation:

Cover the bulletin board with yellow or gold mural paper.

Optional: Print enough copies of the *Board 4 Colored Pencil Border* to frame the bulletin board. Cut the borders in half. Staple or glue the border to the bulletin board (see sample board).

Print *Board 4 Title.* Staple or glue the title to the bulletin board (see sample board).

Print *Board 4 Self Quotation 6.* Staple or glue the quotation to the bulletin board (see sample board).

Print a red, blue, or green *Board 4 Picture Frame* for each student.

Optional: Print copies of the *Board 4 Star Patterns.* Cut out the stars to decorate the board (see sample board).

Directions:

Explain that each student is a one-of-a kind, unique person. Give each student a *Board 4 Picture Frame*, scissors, and crayons, markers, or colored pencils to draw a self-portrait.

Optional: Provide mirrors. Remind the students to use the correct colors for eyes, hair, and skin. (Young children tend to grab the first crayon they find.)

Optional: Students cut out their picture frames. (Note: This will let you fit more frames on the bulletin board.)

Glue or staple the completed drawings around the bulletin board title.

Students try to find their own pictures. Can they find their friends' pictures? Emphasize that every picture is a unique, one-of-a-kind masterpiece.

COUNSELING ON THE WALL! © 2009 MAR✳CO PRODUCTS, INC. 1-800-448-2197

UNIT 2

Attitude

There are more quotations by famous people on the need to have confidence than on any other topic. Children, as well as adults, need to be reminded that a good attitude is essential to achieving goals and finding success in school as well as in life. The feeling of confidence is necessary before a person can begin to learn goal-setting steps. Affirmations remind us all to check our attitudes. What a great opportunity for some *Counseling On The Wall!*

ASCA STANDARDS
FOR UNIT 2—ATTITUDE

ACADEMIC DEVELOPMENT	
Standard A: Students will acquire the attitudes, knowledge and skills that contribute to effective learning in school and across the life span.	
A:A1	**Improve Academic Self-Concept**
A:A1.1	Articulate feelings of competence and confidence as learners
A:A1.2	Display a positive interest in learning
A:A1.3	Take pride in work and achievement
A:A1.4	Accept mistakes as essential to the learning process
A:A1.5	Identify attitudes and behaviors that lead to successful learning
Standard B: Students will complete school with the academic preparation essential to choose from a wide range of substantial post- secondary options, including college.	
A:B1	**Improve Learning**
A:B1.1	Demonstrate the motivation to achieve individual potential
A:B2	**Plan To Achieve Goals**
A:B2.6	Understand the relationship between classroom performance and success in school

PERSONAL/SOCIAL DEVELOPMENT	
Standard A: Students will acquire the knowledge, attitudes and interpersonal skills to help them understand and respect self and others.	
PS:A1	**Acquire Self-Knowledge**
PS:A1.2	Identify values, attitudes and beliefs
Standard B: Students will make decisions, set goals and take necessary action to achieve goals.	
PS:B1	**Self-Knowledge Application**
PS:B1.11	Use persistence and perseverance in acquiring knowledge and skills

COUNSELING ON THE WALL! © 2009 MAR★CO PRODUCTS, INC. 1-800-448-2197

ATTITUDE IS EVERYTHING!

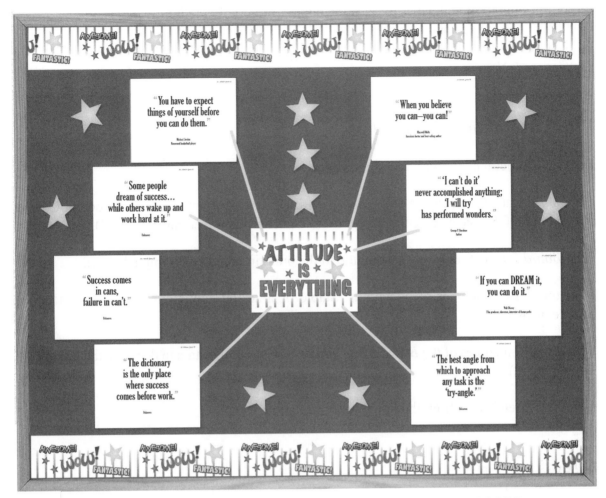

SAMPLE BOARD IS BASED ON A 5' WIDE X 4' TALL BULLETIN BOARD

Objective: To enable students to identify attitudes and behaviors that lead to success in school and in life

Time: One 40-60 minute class period

Materials Needed:

For the leader:
☐ Red mural paper for the bulletin board background
☐ *Optional: Board 5 Wow Border* cut in half (included on CD)
☐ *Board 5 Title* (included on CD) or make the title from purchased bulletin board letters

COUNSELING ON THE WALL! © 2009 MAR★CO PRODUCTS, INC. 1-800-448-2197

☐ Selected *Board 5 Quotations About Attitude* (included on CD)
☐ *Optional: Board 5 Star Patterns* cut out (included on CD)
☐ White and/or colored paper for printing copies, preferably medium-weight
☐ Stapler and staples or glue
☐ Scissors
☐ *Optional:* Yarn

Pre-Presentation Preparation:

Cover the bulletin board with red mural paper.

Optional: Print enough copies of the *Board 5 Wow Border* to frame the bulletin board. Cut the borders in half. Staple or glue the border to the bulletin board (see sample board).

Print *Board 5 Title*. Staple or glue the title to the bulletin board (see sample board).

Print the desired number of quotations. Staple or glue the quotations around the title (see sample board).

Optional: Print copies of the *Board 5 Star Patterns*. Cut out the stars to decorate the board (see sample board).

Optional: Stretch yarn from the title to each quotation.

Directions:

Tell the students that the purpose of the lesson is to learn about attitudes and behaviors that will help them be successful. Since quotations often facilitate this process, this lesson focuses on the sayings on the bulletin board.

Call attention to the bulletin board title. Ask several students to explain what the title means to them.

Read the quotations aloud or ask the students to read them silently. Have volunteers select a quotation and explain why they believe it pertains to attitude.

COUNSELING ON THE WALL! © 2009 MAR✶CO PRODUCTS, INC. 1-800-448-2197

SUCCESS COMES IN CANS

SAMPLE BOARD IS BASED ON A 5′ WIDE X 4′ TALL BULLETIN BOARD

Objective: To help students learn how effort and persistence positively affect learning

Time: One 40-60 minute class period

Materials Needed:

For the leader:

☐ Blue mural paper for the bulletin board background

☐ *Optional: Board 6 Can Border* cut in half (included on CD)

☐ *Board 6 Title* (included on CD) or make the title from purchased bulletin board letters

☐ *Board 6 Cans* cut out (included on CD)

- ☐ White and/or colored paper for printing copies, preferably medium-weight
- ☐ Stapler and staples or glue
- ☐ Scissors
- ☐ *Optional:* Yarn

Pre-Presentation Preparation:

Cover the bulletin board with blue mural paper.

Optional: Print enough copies of the *Board 6 Can Border* to frame the bulletin board. Cut the borders in half. Staple or glue the border to the bulletin board (see sample board).

Print *Board 6 Title*. Staple or glue the title to the bulletin board (see sample board).

Print and cut out *Board 6 Cans*. (*Note*: Feel free to add your own words on the blank can shape.) Staple or glue the cans around the title (see sample board).

Directions:

Students read the words on the cans. Ask what they'd like to accomplish in school this year. Remind them that they *CAN DO* more with a *CAN DO* attitude.

COUNSELING ON THE WALL! © 2009 MAR∗CO PRODUCTS, INC. 1-800-448-2197

"TRY ANGLE"

SAMPLE BOARD IS BASED ON A 5′ WIDE X 4′ TALL BULLETIN BOARD

Objective: To help students learn that mistakes are a normal part of the learning process and to understand that words of encouragement will help them overcome mistakes

Time: One 40-60 minute class period

Materials Needed:

For the leader:
- ☐ Blue mural paper for the bulletin board background
- ☐ *Optional: Board 7 Triangle Border* cut in half (included on CD)
- ☐ *Board 7 Title* (included on CD) or make the title from purchased bulletin board letters

- [ ] *Board 7 Triangles* cut out (included on CD)
- [ ] White and/or colored paper for printing copies, preferably medium-weight
- [ ] Stapler and staples or glue
- [ ] Scissors

Pre-Presentation Preparation:

Cover the bulletin board with blue mural paper.

Optional: Print enough copies of the *Board 7 Triangle Border* to frame the bulletin board. Cut the borders in half. Staple or glue the border to the bulletin board (see sample board).

Print *Board 7 Title.* (*Note*: This is *Attitude Quotation 8* from Bulletin Board 5.) Staple or glue the title to the bulletin board (see sample board).

Print and cut out *Board 7 Triangles*. (*Note*: Feel free to add your own words on the blank triangle shape.) Staple or glue the triangles around the title (see sample board).

Directions:

Tell the students that although tough tasks sometimes seem overwhelming, a good attitude will help them overcome obstacles. Remind them to encourage themselves with such positive daily self-messages as: "I will keep trying!" and "I can do it!"

COUNSELING ON THE WALL! © 2009 MAR∗CO PRODUCTS, INC. 1-800-448-2197

OUR DREAMS FOR THE FUTURE ...

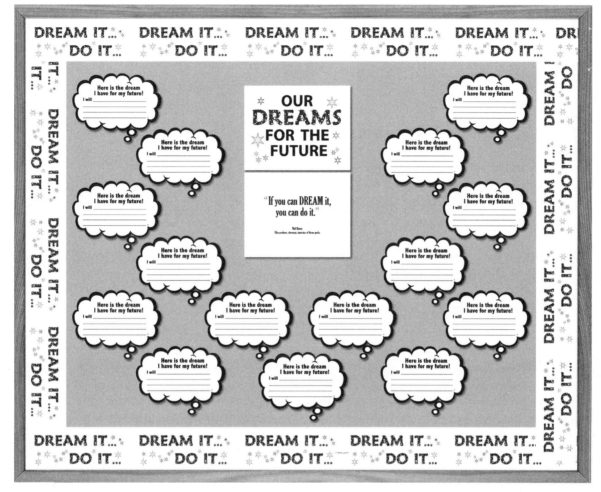

SAMPLE BOARD IS BASED ON A 5' WIDE X 4' TALL BULLETIN BOARD

Objective: To make students aware of the relationship between education and achieving long-term goals

Time: One 40-60 minute class period

Materials Needed:

For the leader:

☐ Yellow mural paper for the bulletin board background

☐ *Optional: Board 8 Dream Border* cut in half (included on CD)

☐ *Board 8 Title* (included on CD) or make the title from purchased bulletin board letters

☐ *Board 8 Attitude Quotation 7* (included on CD)

☐ White and/or colored paper for printing copies, preferably medium-weight

COUNSELING ON THE WALL! © 2009 MAR✷CO PRODUCTS, INC. 1-800-448-2197

☐ Stapler and staples or glue
☐ Scissors

For each student:
☐ *Board 8 Thought Bubble* for each student (included on CD)
☐ Pencil
☐ *Optional:* Scissors

Pre-Presentation Preparation:

Cover the bulletin board with yellow mural paper.

Optional: Print enough copies of the *Board 8 Dream Border* to frame the bulletin board. Cut the borders in half. Staple or glue the border to the bulletin board (see sample board).

Print *Board 8 Title* and the *Board 8 Attitude Quotation 7.* Staple or glue the title and quotation to the bulletin board (see sample board).

Print a *Thought Bubble* (with or without the sentence starter) for each student.

Directions:

When presenting a lesson on the importance of having a *CAN DO* attitude, mention Walt Disney as a good example of someone who had big dreams and achieved big results. He won 26 Oscars for his films; 7 Emmy Awards for TV; created Mickey Mouse, Donald Duck, Pluto, and other world-famous cartoon characters; and designed Disneyland® and Walt Disney World® in the United States and theme parks in Japan, France, and China. Aren't we glad Walt Disney had big dreams?

Tell the students you'd like them to dream big and that you'd like to put their dreams on a special bulletin board with a quotation from Walt Disney. Point to *Attitude Quotation 7* and read it aloud with the students.

Give each student a *Thought Bubble* and a pencil. If the students will be cutting out the *Thought Bubble*, distribute scissors. Have each student complete the sentence starter: "Here is the dream I have for my future. I will _____." Or have the students write their ideas in the blank *Thought Bubble.*

Be sure the students put their names on their paper.

Attach the students' thought bubbles to the bulletin board.

Tell the students that writing down a dream for the future is also called setting a long-term goal. Long-term goals must be broken into smaller, short-term goals. Tell the students to break their future dreams into short-term goals and begin working to accomplish these smaller goals.

COUNSELING ON THE WALL! © 2009 MAR✶CO PRODUCTS, INC. 1-800-448-2197

UNIT 3

Goal-Setting

It is important that children learn to set and attain goals. People of all ages are more successful if they set realistic and measurable long-term goals and break them into attainable short-term goals. This unit's quotations and bulletin board ideas remind students that goal-setting is the key to success.

ASCA STANDARDS
FOR UNIT 3—GOAL-SETTING

ACADEMIC DEVELOPMENT	
Standard A: Students will acquire the attitudes, knowledge and skills that contribute to effective learning in school and across the life span.	
A:A1	**Improve Academic Self-concept**
A:A1.5	Identify attitudes and behaviors that lead to successful learning
A:A3	**Achieve School Success**
A:A3.1	Take responsibility for their actions
Standard B: Students will complete school with the academic preparation essential to choose from a wide range of substantial post- secondary options, including college.	
A:B1	**Improve Learning**
A:B1.7	Become a self-directed and independent learner
A:B2	**Plan To Achieve Goals**
A:B2.6	Understand the relationship between classroom performance and success in school

CAREER DEVELOPMENT	
Standard A: Students will acquire the skills to investigate the world of work in relation to knowledge of self and to make informed career decisions.	
C:A1	**Develop Career Awareness**
C:A1.6	Learn how to set goals
C:A1.7	Understand the importance of planning

PERSONAL/SOCIAL DEVELOPMENT	
Standard A: Students will acquire the knowledge, attitudes and interpersonal skills to help them understand and respect self and others.	
PS:A1	**Acquire Self-Knowledge**
PS:A1.1	Develop positive attitudes toward self as a unique and worthy person
PS:A1.3	Learn the goal-setting process
Standard B: Students will make decisions, set goals and take necessary action to achieve goals.	
PS:B1	**Self-Knowledge Application**
PS:B1.2	Understand consequences of decisions and choices
PS:B1.9	Identify long- and short-term goals
PS:B1.10	Identify alternative ways of achieving goals

COUNSELING ON THE WALL! © 2009 MAR✶CO PRODUCTS, INC. 1-800-448-2197

SETTING HIGH GOALS
IS THE KEY TO SUCCESS!

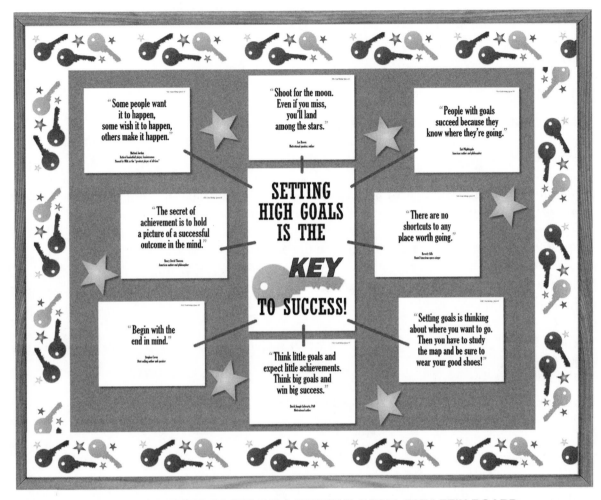

SAMPLE BOARD IS BASED ON A 5′ WIDE X 4′ TALL BULLETIN BOARD

Objective: To help students understand the importance of planning and setting long-term goals

Time: One 40-60 minute class period

Materials Needed:

For the leader:
☐ Green mural paper for the bulletin board background
☐ *Optional: Board 9 Key Border* cut in half (included on CD)

33

- ☐ *Board 9 Title* (included on CD) or make the title from purchased bulletin board letters
- ☐ Selected *Board 9 Goal-Setting Quotations* (included on CD)
- ☐ *Optional: Board 9 Star Patterns* cut out (included on CD)
- ☐ White and/or colored paper for printing copies, preferably medium-weight
- ☐ Stapler and staples or glue
- ☐ Scissors
- ☐ *Optional:* Yarn

Pre-Presentation Preparation:

Cover the bulletin board with green mural paper.

Optional: Print enough copies of the *Board 9 Key Border* to frame the bulletin board. Cut the borders in half. Staple or glue the border to the bulletin board (see sample board).

Print *Board 9 Title*. Staple or glue the title to the bulletin board (see sample board).

Print the desired number of quotations. Staple or glue the quotations around the title (see sample board).

Optional: Print copies of the *Board 9 Star Patterns*. Cut out the stars to decorate the board (see sample board).

Optional: Stretch yarn from the title to each quotation.

Directions:

Tell the students that a reminder about setting and reaching goals will keep goal-setting in their minds. Have each student select one quotation. Print each selected quotation for the student to take home and post in his/her room.

COUNSELING ON THE WALL! © 2009 MAR∗CO PRODUCTS, INC. 1-800-448-2197

SHOOT FOR THE MOON

SAMPLE BOARD IS BASED ON A 5' WIDE X 4' TALL BULLETIN BOARD

Objective: To help students learn the importance of establishing challenging academic goals

Time: One 40-60 minute class period

Materials Needed:

For the leader:

☐ Dark blue mural paper for the bulletin board background

☐ *Optional: Board 10 Space Border* cut in half (included on CD)

☐ *Board 10 Rocket* cut out (included on CD)

☐ *Board 10 Moon* cut out (included on CD)
☐ *Board 10 Goal Setting Stars* cut out (included on CD)
☐ White and/or colored paper for printing copies, preferably medium-weight
☐ Stapler and staples or glue
☐ Scissors

Pre-Presentation Preparation:

Cover the bulletin board with dark blue mural paper.

Optional: Print enough copies of the *Board 10 Space Border* to frame the bulletin board. Cut the borders in half. Staple or glue the border to the bulletin board (see sample board).

Print *Board 10 Rocket* and cut it out. Staple or glue the rocket to the bulletin board (see sample board).

Print *Board 10 Moon* and cut it out. Staple or glue the moon to the bulletin board (see sample board).

Print *Board 10 Goal Setting Stars* and cut them out. Staple or glue the stars to the bulletin board (see sample board). (*Note*: Feel free to add your own goal-word suggestions on blank stars.)

Directions:

Review the goal words on the bulletin board and have each student select one as his/her personal goal.

COUNSELING ON THE WALL! © 2009 MAR✴CO PRODUCTS, INC. 1-800-448-2197

WHERE DO YOU WANT TO GO?

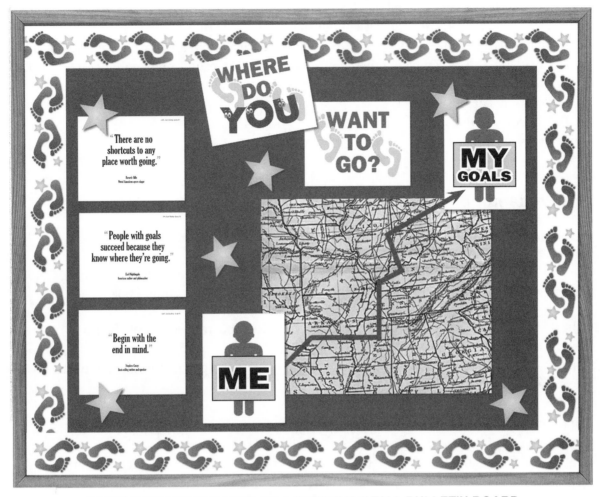

SAMPLE BOARD IS BASED ON A 5' WIDE X 4' TALL BULLETIN BOARD

Objective: : To help students understand the relationship between educational achievement and career success

Time: One 40-60 minute class period

Materials Needed:

For the leader:

☐ Red mural paper for the bulletin board background

☐ *Optional: Board 11 Feet Border* cut in half (included on CD)

☐ *Board 11 Title* (included on CD) or make the title from purchased bulletin board letters

37

- ☐ *Board 11 Goal Quotations 3-5* (included on CD)
- ☐ *Board 11 Me* (included on CD)
- ☐ *Board 11 My Goals* (included on CD)
- ☐ *Optional: Board 11 Star Patterns* cut out (included on CD)
- ☐ Road map (*Note:* Maps may be obtained on the Internet or a map can be purchased if funds are available. Maps can be purchased at service stations, drug stores, dollar stores, etc.)
- ☐ White and/or colored paper for printing copies, preferably medium-weight
- ☐ Stapler and staples or glue
- ☐ Bright-colored marker
- ☐ Scissors

Pre-Presentation Preparation:

Cover the bulletin board with red mural paper.

Optional: Print enough copies of the *Board 11 Feet Border* to frame the bulletin board. Cut the borders in half. Staple or glue the border to the bulletin board (see sample board).

Print *Board 11 Title*. Staple or glue the title to the bulletin board (see sample board).

Print *Board 11 Goal Quotations 3-5*. Staple or glue the quotations to the left side of the board (see sample board).

Staple or glue the road map to the bulletin board (see sample board).

Print *Board 11 Me* and *Board 11 My Goals*. Staple or glue the *Me* to the lower left corner of the map. Attach *My Goals* to the upper right corner of the map (see sample board).

Using the marker, trace a path across the map.

Optional: Print copies of the *Board 11 Star Patterns*. Cut out the stars to decorate the board (see sample board).

Directions:

Remind the students that succeeding in school or in any area of life requires being clear on where they want to go. Goal-setting will help them stay on the right path.

COUNSELING ON THE WALL! © 2009 MAR*CO PRODUCTS, INC. 1-800-448-2197

THE SKY IS THE LIMIT

SAMPLE BOARD IS BASED ON A 5′ WIDE X 4′ TALL BULLETIN BOARD

Objective: To help students understand that an annual plan of study will maximize academic ability and achievement

Time: One 40-60 minute class period

Materials Needed:

For the leader:
☐ Dark blue mural paper for the bulletin board background
☐ *Board 12 Title* (included on CD) or make the title from purchased bulletin board letters
☐ *Board 12 Rocket Ship* cut out (included on CD)
☐ *Board 12 Earth* cut out (included on CD)

COUNSELING ON THE WALL! © **2009** MAR✴CO PRODUCTS, INC. 1-800-448-2197

- ☐ *Board 12 Planets* cut out (included on CD)
- ☐ White and/or colored paper for printing copies, preferably medium-weight
- ☐ Scissors
- ☐ Stapler and staples or glue
- ☐ Bright-colored marker

For each student:
- ☐ *Board 12 Goal-Setting Star* (included on CD)
- ☐ Crayons or markers
- ☐ Pencil
- ☐ Scissors

Pre-Presentation Preparation:

Cover the bulletin board with dark blue mural paper.

Print *Board 12 Title*. Staple or glue the title to the bulletin board (see sample board).

Print and cut out *Board 12 Rocket Ship*. Staple or glue the rocket ship to the bulletin board (see sample board).

Print and cut out *Board 12 Earth*. Staple or glue the earth to the bulletin board (see sample board).

Print and cut out *Board 12 Planets*. Staple or glue the planets to the bulletin board (see sample board).

Print a *Board 12 Goal-Setting Star* (with or without the sentence starter) for each student. *Optional:* Cut out the stars prior to the lesson.

Directions:

Teach a lesson on goal-setting.

Give each student a copy of the *Board 12 Goal-Setting Star*, a pencil, crayons or markers, and scissors. Remind the students that their goals should be realistic and measurable. Have students use the sentence starter: "By the end of the year, I will _____." Or have the students write their ideas on the blank *Star Shape*.

Students sign, decorate, and cut out their stars. Cover as much of the bulletin board as possible with the students' completed stars.

Remind the students that hard work, determination, and a good attitude can accomplish any goal. Ask why *The Sky Is The Limit* is a great name for a bulletin board on goal-setting.

COUNSELING ON THE WALL! © 2009 MAR✶CO PRODUCTS, INC. 1-800-448-2197

UNIT 4

Perseverance

Guidance curriculums frequently describe perseverance as a sub-category of character education. Because perseverance is often the key to success, *Counseling On The Wall!* highlights this essential trait in a separate unit.

A student who starts with a good attitude and sets clear and measurable goals may fail if he/she lacks the resolve and determination to persist in the face of adversity.

To encourage students to practice perseverance, create bulletin boards that remind everyone that successful people keep trying even when tasks seems daunting and results are not instantaneous.

ASCA STANDARDS
FOR UNIT 4—PERSEVERANCE

ACADEMIC DEVELOPMENT	
Standard A: Students will acquire the attitudes, knowledge and skills that contribute to effective learning in school and across the life span.	
A:A1	**Improve Academic Self-concept**
A:A1.4	Accept mistakes as essential to the learning process
A:A1.5	Identify attitudes and behaviors that lead to successful learning
A:A3	**Achieve School Success**
A:A3.1	Take responsibility for their actions
Standard B: Students will complete school with the academic preparation essential to choose from a wide range of substantial post- secondary options, including college.	
A:B2	**Plan To Achieve Goals**
A:B2.6	Understand the relationship between classroom performance and success in school
Standard C: Students will understand the relationship of academics to the world of work and to life at home and in the community.	
A:C1	**Relate School To Life Experiences**
A:C1.5	Understand that school success is the preparation to make the transition from student to community member

PERSONAL/SOCIAL DEVELOPMENT	
Standard A: Students will acquire the knowledge, attitudes and interpersonal skills to help them understand and respect self and others.	
PS:A1	**Acquire Self-Knowledge**
PS:A1.1	Develop positive attitudes toward self as a unique and worthy person
PS:A1.3	Learn the goal-setting process
Standard B: Students will make decisions, set goals and take necessary action to achieve goals.	
PS:B1	**Self-Knowledge Application**
PS:B1.2	Understand consequences of decisions and choices
PS:B1.9	Identify long- and short-term goals
PS:B1.10	Identify alternative ways of achieving goals

COUNSELING ON THE WALL! © 2009 MAR★CO PRODUCTS, INC. 1-800-448-2197

KEEP TRYING...THAT'S PERSEVERANCE!

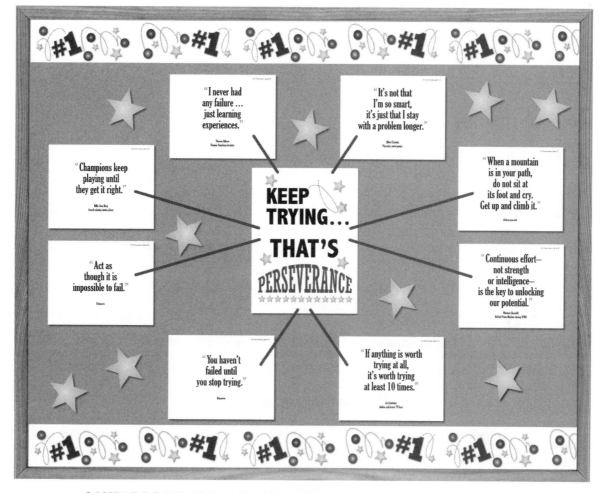

SAMPLE BOARD IS BASED ON A 5' WIDE X 4' TALL BULLETIN BOARD

Objective: To help students understand that winners keep trying, even when tasks seems daunting and results are not instantaneous

Time: One 40-60 minute class period

Materials Needed:

For the leader:
☐ Blue mural paper for the bulletin board background
☐ *Optional: Board 13 Number One Border* cut in half (included on CD)
☐ *Board 13 Title* (included on CD) or make the title from purchased bulletin board letters

43

☐ Selected *Board 13 Perseverance Quotations* (included on CD)
☐ *Optional: Board 13 Star Patterns* cut out (included on CD)
☐ White and/or colored paper for printing copies, preferably medium-weight
☐ Stapler and staples or glue
☐ Scissors
☐ *Optional:* Yarn

Pre-Presentation Preparation:

Cover the bulletin board with blue mural paper.

Optional: Print enough copies of the *Board 13 Number One Border* to frame the bulletin board. Cut the borders in half. Staple or glue the border to the bulletin board (see sample board).

Print *Board 13 Title*. Staple or glue the title to the bulletin board (see sample board).

Print the desired number of quotations. Staple or glue the quotations around the title (see sample board).

Optional: Print copies of the *Board 13 Star Patterns*. Cut out the stars to decorate the board (see sample board).

Optional: Stretch yarn from the title to each quotation.

Directions:

Review the quotations. Have each student select and share with the group the quotation he/she believes would most inspire him/her to persevere.

COUNSELING ON THE WALL! © 2009 MAR★CO PRODUCTS, INC. 1-800-448-2197

PERSEVERANCE PAYS OFF!

SAMPLE BOARD IS BASED ON A 5′ WIDE X 4′ TALL BULLETIN BOARD

Objective: To help students understand how effort and persistence positively affect learning

Time: One 40-60 minute class period

Materials Needed:

For the leader:

☐ Red mural paper for the bulletin board background

☐ *Optional: Board 14 Money Border* cut in half (included on CD)

☐ *Board 14 Title* (included on CD) or make the title from purchased bulletin board letters

- [ ] *Board 14 Perseverance Money* cut out (included on CD)
- [ ] White and/or colored paper for printing copies, preferably medium-weight
- [ ] Stapler and staples or glue
- [ ] Scissors

Pre-Presentation Preparation:

Cover the bulletin board with red mural paper.

Optional: Print enough copies of the *Board 14 Money Border* to frame the bulletin board. Cut the borders in half. Staple or glue the border to the bulletin board (see sample board).

Print *Board 14 Title*. Staple or glue the title to the bulletin board (see sample board).

Print *Board 14 Perseverance Money*. Cut out the dollar bills to decorate the board (see sample board). (*Note*: Feel free to add your own words of encouragement to the blank dollar bill shapes.)

Directions:

Discuss the relationship of words of encouragement to perseverance. Ask why and how perseverance can pay off.

COUNSELING ON THE WALL! © 2009 MAR✶CO PRODUCTS, INC. 1-800-448-2197

CHAMPIONS KEEP PLAYING!

SAMPLE BOARD IS BASED ON A 5' WIDE X 4' TALL BULLETIN BOARD

Objective: To help students understand how continued effort influences success in school and in life

Time: One 40-60 minute class period

Materials Needed:

For the leader:

☐ Blue mural paper for the bulletin board background

☐ *Optional: Board 15 Trophy Border* cut in half (included on CD)

☐ *Board 15 Title* (included on CD) or make the title from purchased bulletin board letters

☐ White and/or colored paper for printing copies, preferably medium-weight
☐ Stapler and staples or glue
☐ Scissors

For each student:
☐ *Board 15 Trophy* (included on CD)
☐ Pencil
☐ *Optional:* Scissors
☐ *Optional:* Glitter and glue

Pre-Presentation Preparation:

Cover the bulletin board with blue mural paper.

Optional: Print enough copies of the *Board 15 Trophy Border* to frame the bulletin board. Cut the borders in half. Staple or glue the border to the bulletin board (see sample board).

Print *Board 15 Title*. (*Note*: This is *Perseverance Quotation 5* from Bulletin Board 13.) Staple or glue the title to the bulletin board (see sample board).

Print a *Board 15 Trophy* (with or without the sentence starter) for each student. *Optional:* Cut out the trophies prior to the lesson.

Directions:

Conduct a classroom lesson on perseverance, sharing *Perseverance Quotation 5* with the students. Explain that this is a good rule to live by in all endeavors. Ask:

> *How many of you would like to be champions?*

Tell the students they already are champions! Say:

> *Although you'll have lots of new challenges this year in school, I know you'll succeed. Your past behavior has proven that you're all champions.*

> *Think about something you can do because you tried and tried and practiced and practiced. You showed perseverance!*

You may spend time sharing these victories.

COUNSELING ON THE WALL! © 2009 MAR★CO PRODUCTS, INC. 1-800-448-2197

Tell the students you're going to give trophies for their accomplishments. Give each student a copy of the *Board 15 Trophy*, a pencil, scissors, and (optional) glitter and glue. Have the students complete the sentence starter: "Once I didn't know how to _____, but I kept trying and now I can _____." Or have them write their ideas on the blank trophy. (*Note:* Older students can be encouraged to write in more detail, explaining what they did to learn and how they kept going even when the task was difficult.)

Students sign, decorate, and cut out their trophies. Attach the completed trophies to the board.

Give the students time to share trophy accomplishments with the class. Ask how past accomplishments can relate to future accomplishments. (Example: *Once I didn't know how to add, but I kept trying. I can do it now, so I know I can learn multiplication this year!*)

COUNSELING ON THE WALL! © 2009 MAR✳CO PRODUCTS, INC. 1-800-448-2197

UNIT 5

Friendship

A child who learns to be a good friend at an early age will develop life-long relationships and be happier and more successful at school and in life. This unit's bulletin boards reinforce the idea that to *have* friends, you must *be* a friend.

ASCA STANDARDS
FOR UNIT 5—FRIENDSHIP

PERSONAL/SOCIAL DEVELOPMENT	
Standard A: Students will acquire the knowledge, attitudes and interpersonal skills to help them understand and respect self and others.	
PS:A2	**Acquire Interpersonal Skills**
PS:A2.1	Recognize that everyone has rights and responsibilities
PS:A2.2	Respect alternative points of view
PS:A2.3	Recognize, accept, respect and appreciate individual differences
PS:A2.4	Recognize, accept and appreciate ethnic and cultural diversity
PS:A2.7	Know that communication involves speaking, listening and nonverbal behavior

COUNSELING ON THE WALL! © 2009 MAR✷CO PRODUCTS, INC. 1-800-448-2197

EVERYBODY NEEDS FRIENDS

SAMPLE BOARD IS BASED ON A 5′ WIDE X 4′ TALL BULLETIN BOARD

Objective: To help students understand the importance of making and keeping friends

Time: One 40-60 minute class period

Materials Needed:

For the leader:

☐ Dark blue mural paper for the bulletin board background

☐ *Optional: Board 16 Kids Border* cut in half (included on CD)

☐ *Board 16 Title* (included on CD) or make the title from purchased bulletin board letters

☐ Selected *Board 16 Friendship Quotations* (included on CD)

- ☐ *Optional: Board 16 Stars* cut out (included on CD)
- ☐ White and/or colored paper for printing copies, preferably medium-weight
- ☐ Stapler and staples or glue
- ☐ Scissors
- ☐ *Optional:* Yarn

Pre-Presentation Preparation:

Cover the bulletin board with dark blue mural paper.

Optional: Print enough copies of the *Board 16 Kids Border* to frame the bulletin board. Cut the borders in half. Staple or glue the border to the bulletin board (see sample board).

Print *Board 16 Title*. Staple or glue the title to the bulletin board (see sample board).

Print the desired number of quotations. Staple or glue the quotations around the title (see sample board).

Optional: Print copies of the *Board 16 Stars*. Cut out the stars to decorate the board (see sample board).

Optional: Stretch yarn from the title to each quotation.

Directions:

Review the selected quotations, explaining how they relate to the importance of having friends. If time permits, have students create new quotations about *friendship*.

FRIENDSHIP IS A GIFT

SAMPLE BOARD IS BASED ON A 5′ WIDE X 4′ TALL BULLETIN BOARD

Objective: To help students clarify values, attitudes, and beliefs about the importance of interacting with others and forming friendships

Time: One 40-60 minute class period

Materials Needed:

For the leader:

☐ Yellow mural paper for the bulletin board background

☐ *Optional: Board 17 Gifts Border* cut in half (included on CD)

☐ *Board 17 Title* (included on CD) or make the title from purchased bulletin board letters

- ☐ *Board 17 Friendship Quotation 5* (included on CD)
- ☐ White and/or colored paper for printing copies, preferably medium-weight
- ☐ *Option 1:* Strong double-sided tape to fasten the packages on the board
- ☐ *Option 2:* Large pieces of ribbon and a large bow
- ☐ Stapler and staples or glue
- ☐ Scissors
- ☐ *Optional:* Bows

For each student:
- ☐ *Option 1:* Small box, wrapping paper, scissors, tape, and a bow

Pre-Presentation Preparation:

Cover the bulletin board with yellow mural paper.

Optional: Print enough copies of the *Board 17 Gifts Border* to frame the bulletin board. Cut the borders in half. Staple or glue the border to the bulletin board (see sample board).

Print *Board 18 Title*. Staple or glue the title to the bulletin board (see sample board).

Print *Board 17 Friendship Quotation 5*. Staple or glue the quotation to the bulletin board (see sample board).

Directions:

Option 1: Give each student a small box, wrapping paper, scissors, tape, and a bow. Students wrap their boxes and attach the bows. Randomly tape the boxes to the bulletin board. (*Note:* The leader or student assistants may make these boxes in advance.) Each student writes his/her name on his/her box.

Option 2: If you're not using gift boxes, decorate the bulletin board with two large ribbons. Attach a large bow to the center of the board, where the ribbons cross.

Ask the students to explain the meaning of the quotation. Discuss what a person must do in order to receive the gift of friendship.

Optional: Decorate the board with bows.

COUNSELING ON THE WALL! © 2009 MAR✶CO PRODUCTS, INC. 1-800-448-2197

FRIENDSHIP IS THE GOLDEN THREAD

SAMPLE BOARD IS BASED ON A 5' WIDE X 4' TALL BULLETIN BOARD

Objective: To help students understand that forming friendships will provide them someone to play with, someone to talk with, and someone who understands their feelings

Time: One 40-60 minute class period

Materials Needed:

For the leader:
- ☐ Blue mural paper for the bulletin board background
- ☐ *Optional: Board 18 Hearts Border* cut in half (included on CD)
- ☐ *Optional:* Large piece of red construction paper

- [ ] *Board 18 Friendship Quotation 1* (included on CD)
- [ ] Scissors
- [ ] Stapler and staples or glue
- [ ] Gold yarn or gold-colored marker

For each student:
- [ ] *Large Heart* (included on CD)
- [ ] Scissors
- [ ] Crayons or markers
- [ ] Pencil

Pre-Presentation Preparation:

Cover the bulletin board with blue mural paper.

Optional: Print enough copies of the *Board 18 Hearts Border* to frame the bulletin board. Cut the borders in half. Staple or glue the border to the bulletin board (see sample board).

Print *Board 18 Friendship Quotation 1*. Staple or glue the quotation to the bulletin board (see sample board). *Optional:* Make a large heart shape out of red construction paper. Glue *Friendship Quotation 1* to the center of the heart, then attach it to the center of the board.

Print a *Large Heart* for each student.

Directions:

Give each student a *Large Heart*, a pencil, scissors, and crayons or markers. After writing his/her name on the heart, each student may decorate it and cut it out.

Staple or glue the students' completed hearts all over the bulletin board, then attach gold-colored yarn from the quotation to many of the hearts. Use more yarn to make sure all hearts are connected in some way. (*Note:* To simplify this step, use a gold-colored marker to draw a line representing the thread connecting the hearts.)

Ask:

> *Why is it so nice to have friends?* (Having a friend gives us someone to play with, someone to talk with, someone to understand our feelings, etc.)

Explain that the author of the quotation used descriptive words to explain friendship. Ask the students to explain the quotation and whether they feel the author did a good job.

COUNSELING ON THE WALL! © 2009 MAR✶CO PRODUCTS, INC. 1-800-448-2197

FRIENDSHIP IS UNIQUE
PERSONALITIES WOVEN TOGETHER

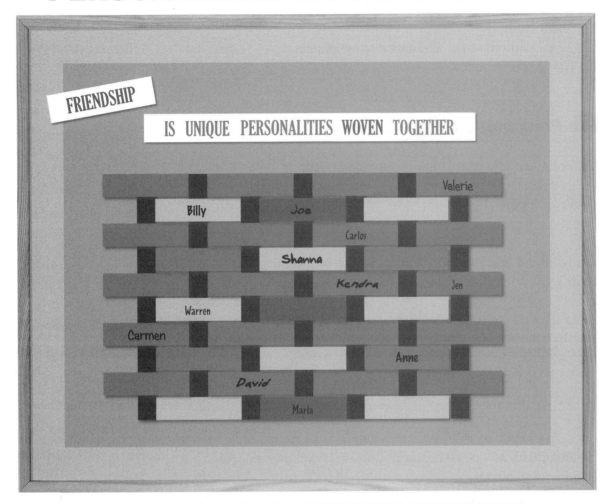

SAMPLE BOARD IS BASED ON A 5′ WIDE X 4′ TALL BULLETIN BOARD

Objective: To help students recognize, accept, respect, and appreciate that individual differences can and should remain intact within friendships

Time: One 40-60 minute class period

Materials Needed:

For the leader:
☐ Green mural paper for the bulletin board background
☐ *Optional:* Border made from gold construction paper

COUNSELING ON THE WALL! © 2009 MAR★CO PRODUCTS, INC. 1-800-448-2197

- ☐ *Board 19 Title* (included on CD) or make the title from purchased bulletin board letters
- ☐ Stapler and staples or glue
- ☐ Scissors

For each student:
- ☐ 2" x 11" piece of colored construction paper
- ☐ Crayons or markers

Pre-Presentation Preparation:

Cover the bulletin board with green mural paper.

Optional: Frame the bulletin board with gold (or another contrasting color) construction paper (see sample board).

Print and cut apart *Board 19 Title*. Staple or glue the title to the bulletin board (see sample board).

Cut a 2" x 11" piece of colored construction paper for each student. Modify the width and length of the strips according to the size of the board and the number of students.

Directions:

Conduct a lesson on *friendship*, explaining that people needn't give up their own uniqueness to get along with others. Brainstorm ideas on how a person could be true to him/herself and still be a friend to others.

Tell the students they're going to help you make beautiful bulletin board.

Give each student a strip of construction paper and crayons or markers to write his/her name on the strip and decorate it however he/she desires.

Weave the decorated strips as if making fabric or a basket. Cover the bulletin board with strips woven over and under each other. Continue until you've used all the strips.

Explain that the woven strips represent the students and their relationships with each other. They are all different, but their uniqueness does not interfere with their ability to be friends.

COUNSELING ON THE WALL! © 2009 MAR✱CO PRODUCTS, INC. 1-800-448-2197

UNIT 6

Cooperation

Because we live, work, and play in groups, learning to cooperate within a group is an important life skill. Successful children and adults recognize a need to get along in a group and have learned that teamwork involves cooperation.

The word cooperation implies that group members have a common goal, have learned to share, take turns, and want to "agree to agree." *Counseling On The Wall!* reinforces these important lessons, which must be taught as part of each year's guidance curriculum.

ASCA STANDARDS FOR UNIT 6—COOPERATION

CAREER DEVELOPMENT	
Standard A: Students will acquire the skills to investigate the world of work in relation to knowledge of self and to make informed career decisions.	
C:A1	**Develop Career Awareness**
C:A1.4	Learn how to interact and work cooperatively in teams
Standard C: Students will understand the relationship between personal qualities, education, training and the world of work.	
C:C2	**Apply Skills to Achieve Career Goals**
C:C2.3	Learn to work cooperatively with others as a team member

PERSONAL/SOCIAL DEVELOPMENT	
Standard A: Students will acquire the knowledge, attitudes and interpersonal skills to help them understand and respect self and others.	
PS:A1	**Acquire Self-Knowledge**
PS:A1.6	Distinguish between appropriate and inappropriate behavior
PS:A1.8	Understand the need for self-control and how to practice it
PS:A2	**Acquire Interpersonal Skills**
PS:A2.1	Recognize that everyone has rights and responsibilities
PS:A2.2	Respect alternative points of view
PS:A2.3	Recognize, accept, respect and appreciate individual differences
PS:A2.4	Recognize, accept and appreciate ethnic and cultural diversity
Standard B: Students will make decisions, set goals and take necessary action to achieve goals.	
PS:B1	**Self-Knowledge Application**
PS:B1.3	Identify alternative solutions to a problem
PS:B1.8	Know when peer pressure is influencing a decision

COUNSELING ON THE WALL! © 2009 MAR✶CO PRODUCTS, INC. 1-800-448-2197

WORKING TOGETHER...
THAT'S COOPERATION

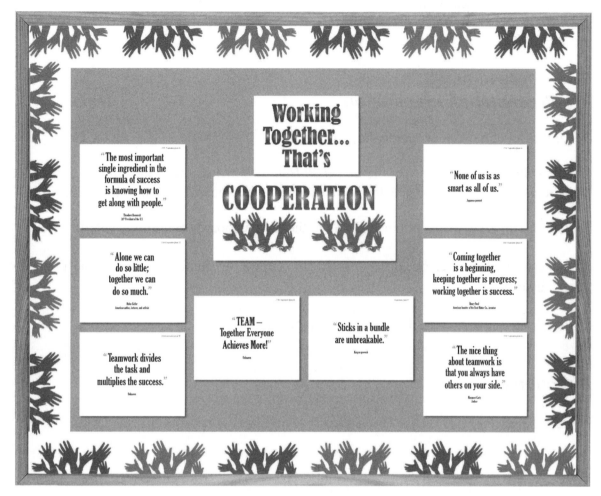

SAMPLE BOARD IS BASED ON A 5' WIDE X 4' TALL BULLETIN BOARD

Objective: To help students learn the importance of teamwork and cooperating with others

Time: One 40-60 minute class period

Materials Needed:

For the leader:
☐ Blue mural paper for the bulletin board background
☐ *Optional: Board 20 Hands Border* cut in half (included on CD)

- ☐ *Board 20 Title* (included on CD) or make the title from purchased bulletin board letters
- ☐ Selected *Board 20 Cooperation Quotations* (included on CD)
- ☐ White and/or colored paper for printing copies, preferably medium-weight
- ☐ Stapler and staples or glue
- ☐ Scissors
- ☐ *Optional:* Yarn

Pre-Presentation Preparation:

Cover the bulletin board with blue mural paper.

Optional: Print enough copies of the *Board 20 Hands Border* to frame the bulletin board. Cut the borders in half. Staple or glue the border to the bulletin board (see sample board).

Print *Board 20 Title*. Staple or glue the title to the bulletin board (see sample board).

Print the desired number of quotations. Staple or glue the quotations around the title (see sample board).

Optional: Stretch yarn from the title to each quotation.

Directions:

Review the selected quotations. Discuss how they relate to *cooperation*.

COUNSELING ON THE WALL! © 2009 MAR∗CO PRODUCTS, INC. 1-800-448-2197

WHEN WE WORK TOGETHER, THE PIECES FIT!

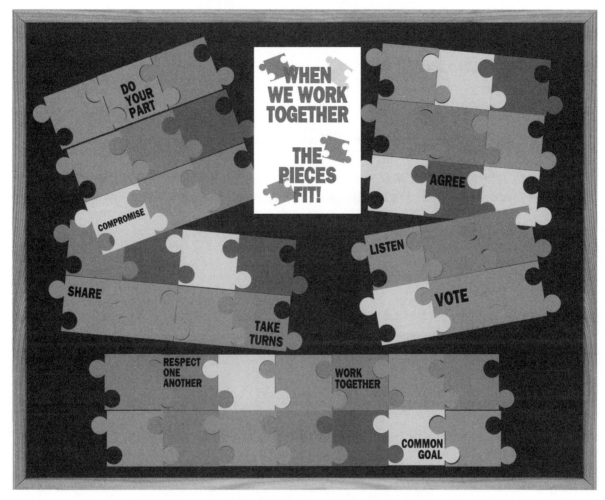

SAMPLE BOARD IS BASED ON A 5′ WIDE X 4′ TALL BULLETIN BOARD

Objective: To introduce students to ways to interact and work cooperatively in teams

Time: One 40-60 minute class period

Materials Needed:

For the leader:
☐ Blue mural paper for the bulletin board background
☐ *Board 21 Title* (included on CD) or make the title from purchased bulletin board letters
☐ *Board 21 Puzzle Pieces* cut out (included on CD)

COUNSELING ON THE WALL! © 2009 MAR✶CO PRODUCTS, INC. 1-800-448-2197

☐ White and/or colored paper for printing copies, preferably medium-weight
☐ Stapler and staples or glue
☐ Scissors
☐ Black marker

Pre-Presentation Preparation:

Cover the bulletin board with blue mural paper.

Print *Board 21 Title*. Staple or glue the title to the bulletin board (see sample board).

Print *Board 21 Puzzle Pieces*. Make several copies of each of the blank puzzle pieces. Cut out the puzzle pieces and staple or glue the interlocking pieces to the bulletin board (see sample board).

Directions:

Review the meaning of each word or phrase and have students explain how each is an example of *cooperation*. (*Note:* Students may fill in empty puzzle pieces with other words or phrases that are examples of *cooperation*.)

COUNSELING ON THE WALL! © 2009 MAR*CO PRODUCTS, INC. 1-800-448-2197

WE ARE A TEAM

SAMPLE BOARD IS BASED ON A 5′ WIDE X 4′ TALL BULLETIN BOARD

Objective: To help students understand that working as a team will improve school atmosphere

Time: One 40-60 minute class period

Materials Needed:

For the leader:
- ☐ Red mural paper for the bulletin board background
- ☐ *Optional: Board 22 Paper Doll Border* cut in half (included on CD)
- ☐ *Board 22 Title* cut in half (included on CD) or make the title from purchased bulletin board letters

COUNSELING ON THE WALL! © 2009 MAR✶CO PRODUCTS, INC. 1-800-448-2197

- ☐ *Board 22 Teamwork Quotations* (included on CD)
- ☐ *Optional: Board 22 Star Patterns* cut out (included on CD)
- ☐ White and/or colored paper for printing copies, preferably medium-weight
- ☐ Stapler and staples or glue
- ☐ Scissors

For each student:
- ☐ *Board 22 Paper Doll* (included on CD)
- ☐ Pencil
- ☐ Crayons or markers
- ☐ Scissors

Pre-Presentation Preparation:

Cover the bulletin board with blue mural paper.

Optional: Print enough copies of the *Board 22 Paper Doll Border* to frame the bulletin board. Cut the borders in half. Staple or glue the border to the bulletin board (see sample board).

Print *Board 22 Title*. Staple or glue the title to the bulletin board (see sample board).

Print *Board 22 Teamwork Quotations*. Staple or glue the quotations to the bulletin board (see sample board).

Print a *Board 22 Paper Doll* for each student.

Optional: Print copies of the *Board 22 Star Patterns*. Cut out the stars to decorate the board (see sample board).

Directions:

Conduct a classroom lesson on *cooperation*, explaining that your school believes in *teamwork*. Discuss this at length, using the term *cooperation*. Tell the students they're going to help you put up a special bulletin board about teamwork.

Give each student a copy of the *Paper Doll*, a pencil, scissors, and crayons or markers. Each student draws a T-shirt on the paper doll, writes his/her name across the middle of the shirt, then the decorates the *Paper Doll* and cuts it out.

Attach the paper dolls, hand to hand, across the board. Use all the paper dolls, making as many lines and as much wall space as needed.

Ask students to suggest different ways they, as a team, could make school a better place. You may want to add your own suggestions.

COUNSELING ON THE WALL! © 2009 MAR✳CO PRODUCTS, INC. 1-800-448-2197

UNIT 7

Kindness

In an elementary guidance curriculum, the need to teach kindness is crucial. Children, who learn to share, smile, and give will be better citizens of the world. It is not always easy for young students to be kind—especially if they're not always treated with kindness. Reminders are important.

ASCA STANDARDS
FOR UNIT 7—KINDNESS

ACADEMIC DEVELOPMENT	
Standard A: Students will acquire the attitudes, knowledge and skills that contribute to effective learning in school and across the life span.	
A:A3	Achieve School Success
A:A3.1	Take responsibility for their actions

CAREER DEVELOPMENT	
Standard A: Students will acquire the skills to investigate the world of work in relation to knowledge of self and to make informed career decisions.	
C:A1	Develop Career Awareness
C:A1.4	Learn how to interact and work cooperatively in teams

PERSONAL/SOCIAL DEVELOPMENT	
Standard A: Students will acquire the knowledge, attitudes and interpersonal skills to help them understand and respect self and others.	
PS:A1	Acquire Self-Knowledge
PS:A1.1	Develop positive attitudes toward self as a unique and worthy person
PS:A1.5	Identify and express feelings
PS:A1.6	Distinguish between appropriate and inappropriate behavior
PS:A2	Acquire Interpersonal Skills
PS:A2.1	Recognize that everyone has rights and responsibilities
PS:A2.2	Respect alternative points of view
PS:A2.3	Recognize, accept, respect and appreciate individual differences
PS:A2.8	Learn how to make and keep friends

COUNSELING ON THE WALL! © 2009 MAR★CO PRODUCTS, INC. 1-800-448-2197

KEEP KINDNESS IN YOUR LIFE

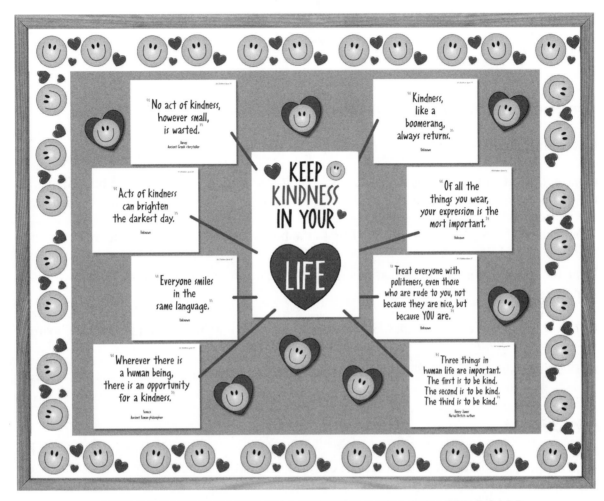

SAMPLE BOARD IS BASED ON A 5′ WIDE X 4′ TALL BULLETIN BOARD

Objective: To help students understand that kindness is a crucial ingredient in creating a positive school environment

Time: One 40-60 minute class period

Materials Needed:

For the leader:
- ☐ Blue mural paper for the bulletin board background
- ☐ *Optional: Board 23 Smile Heart Border* cut in half (included on CD)
- ☐ *Board 23 Title* (included on CD) or make the title from purchased bulletin board letters
- ☐ Selected *Board 23 Kindness Quotations* (included on CD)

☐ *Optional: Board 23 Smiles Hearts* cut out (included on CD)
☐ White and/or colored paper for printing copies, preferably medium-weight
☐ Stapler and staples or glue
☐ Scissors
☐ *Optional:* Yarn

Pre-Presentation Preparation:

Cover the bulletin board with blue mural paper.

Optional: Print enough copies of the *Board 23 Smile Heart Border* to frame the bulletin board. Cut the borders in half. Staple or glue the border to the bulletin board (see sample board).

Print *Board 23 Title*. Staple or glue the title to the bulletin board (see sample board).

Print the desired number of quotations. Staple or glue the quotations around the title (see sample board).

Optional: Print and cut out *Board 23 Smiles Hearts* to decorate the board (see sample board).

Optional: Stretch yarn from the title to each quotation.

Directions:

Review the quotations with the students. Ask each student to share his/her favorite quotation and explain why he/she chose it.

COUNSELING ON THE WALL! © 2009 MAR✶CO PRODUCTS, INC. 1-800-448-2197

ACTS OF KINDNESS CAN BRIGHTEN THE DARKEST DAY

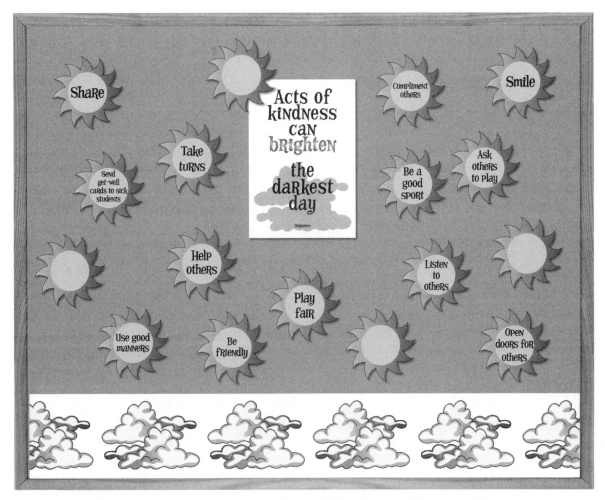

SAMPLE BOARD IS BASED ON A 5' WIDE X 4' TALL BULLETIN BOARD

Objective: To teach students to recognize the components of *kindness*

Time: One 40-60 minute class period

Materials Needed:

For the leader:

☐ Blue mural paper for the bulletin board background

☐ *Optional: Board 24 Clouds Border* (included on CD)

☐ *Board 24 Title* (included on CD) or make the title from purchased bulletin board letters

73

- ☐ *Board 24 Kindness Suns* cut out (included on CD)
- ☐ White and/or colored paper for printing copies, preferably medium-weight
- ☐ Stapler and staples or glue
- ☐ Scissors
- ☐ *Optional:* Gold marker

Pre-Presentation Preparation:

Cover the bulletin board with blue mural paper.

Optional: Print enough copies of *Board 24 Clouds Border* to cover the bottom of the bulletin board. Staple or glue the border to the bulletin board (see sample board).

Print *Board 24 Title*. (*Note*: This is *Kindness Quotation 2* from Bulletin Board 23.) Staple or glue the title to the bulletin board (see sample board).

Print and cut out *Kindness Suns* and attach them to the bulletin board (see sample board). *Optional:* Print several copies of the blank sun.

Optional: Use a gold marker to draw rays of light coming from the suns.

Directions:

Have each student select one act of kindness and commit to performing it for a specified period of time.

(*Note:* Students may fill in blank suns with other words or phrases that are examples of kindness.)

COUNSELING ON THE WALL! © 2009 MAR✶CO PRODUCTS, INC. 1-800-448-2197

THOSE OF US WHO SIGNED, HAVE DECIDED TO BE KIND

SAMPLE BOARD IS BASED ON A 5' WIDE X 4' TALL BULLETIN BOARD

Objective: To help students learn to respect and appreciate individual and cultural differences and recognize the power they have to create a positive school environment

Time: One 40-60 minute class period

Materials Needed:

For the leader:

☐ Blue mural paper for the bulletin board background

☐ *Board 25 Title* (included on CD) or make the title from purchased bulletin board letters

☐ *Optional: Board 25 Large Apple* cut out (included on CD)

COUNSELING ON THE WALL! © 2009 MAR★CO PRODUCTS, INC. 1-800-448-2197

☐ White and/or colored paper for printing copies, preferably medium-weight
☐ Stapler and staples or glue
☐ Scissors
☐ Board and chalk or chartpaper and marker

For each class:
☐ *Board 25 Kindness Contract* (included on CD)

Pre-Presentation Preparation:

Cover the bulletin board with blue mural paper.

Print *Board 25 Title*. Staple or glue the title to the bulletin board (see sample board).

Print one *Board 25 Kindness Contract* for each class.

Optional: Print and cut out several *Board 25 Large Apples* to decorate the bulletin board (see sample board).

Directions:

Schedule a lesson on *kindness* for each class in the school. Since the bulletin board cannot be completed until all classrooms have been seen, conduct all lessons within a short time.

Begin by asking how students would feel about going to a school without insults, teasing, or name-calling—a place where they would hear only kind comments. The students will probably agree it would be wonderful to go to such a school.

Tell the students if they work together toward a common goal and take a kindness pledge, they have the power to make their school the kindest school in the country!

Brainstorm ways students could show kindness toward each other. Write their suggestions on the board/chart paper. Explain that when adults agree to something, they sign a piece of paper and that's what you're asking the students to do.

At the top of each *Kindness Contract*, identify the class. Students from that class who pledge kindness use bright-colored markers to sign the contract.

Attach the signed sheets around the bulletin board title. Leave the bulletin board up for a month. Shortly after taking it down, visit each classroom and ask how students demonstrated kindness. (*Note:* You may do this at the beginning of any classroom guidance lesson.)

COUNSELING ON THE WALL! © 2009 MAR✴CO PRODUCTS, INC. 1-800-448-2197

THE KINDNESS BOARD

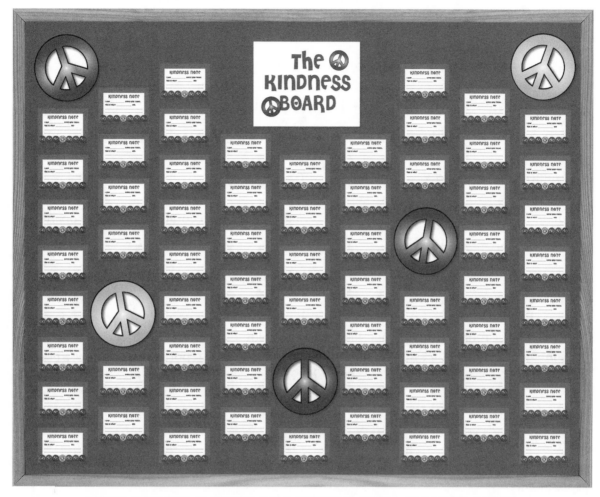

SAMPLE BOARD IS BASED ON A 5' WIDE X 4' TALL BULLETIN BOARD

Objective: To help students recognize that a kindness program can have a positive effect on the school environment and to feel pride in helping accomplish this goal

Time: One 40-60 minute class period

Materials Needed:

For the leader:
☐ Red mural paper for the bulletin board background
☐ *Board 26 Title* (included on CD) or make the title from purchased bulletin board letters
☐ *Board 26 Kindness Notes*, multiple cut-part copies for each class (included on CD)
☐ *Optional: Board 26 Peace Signs* cut out (included on CD)

77

- ☐ White and/or colored paper for printing copies, preferably medium-weight
- ☐ Stapler and staples or glue
- ☐ Scissors

Pre-Presentation Preparation:

Cover the bulletin board with red mural paper.

Print *Board 26 Title*. Staple or glue the title to the bulletin board (see sample board).

Print multiple copies of *Board 26 Kindness Notes* for each class. Cut the notes apart.

Optional: Print and cut out several *Board 26 Peace Signs* to decorate the bulletin board (see sample board).

Directions:

Conduct a classroom lesson about the importance of being kind to friends and even to acquaintances. Explain that random acts of violence are often reported on the news, but that _____ School is ready for some GOOD news!

Tell the students you're creating a special bulletin board to recognize people who are kind and that you'll leave a stack of *Kindness Notes* with their teacher.

A student who performs or observes an act of kindness should write and sign a sentence describing it.

Tell the students how often you'll pick up the notes.

Attach the collected notes to the bulletin board.

Count the number of *Kindness Notes* collected from each classroom. Include the totals in a flier distributed to each classroom, congratulating the students on their achievements and encouraging them to continue their good work.

COUNSELING ON THE WALL! © 2009 MAR✶CO PRODUCTS, INC. 1-800-448-2197

UNIT 8
Feelings

Emotional awareness is key to the development of good emotional health and the secret to a fulfilling life. Children who learn to express feelings appropriately are less likely to become frustrated and to act out in inappropriate ways.

The goal of the elementary counselor should be to help students become aware of their emotions, realize that emotions are based on thoughts, and learn that happiness is often a choice. It is helpful for students to understand that all human beings have comfortable and uncomfortable feelings, but that the choices we make and the ways we react to these feelings can make a difference.

This section's bulletin boards remind students to make good choices when dealing with emotions.

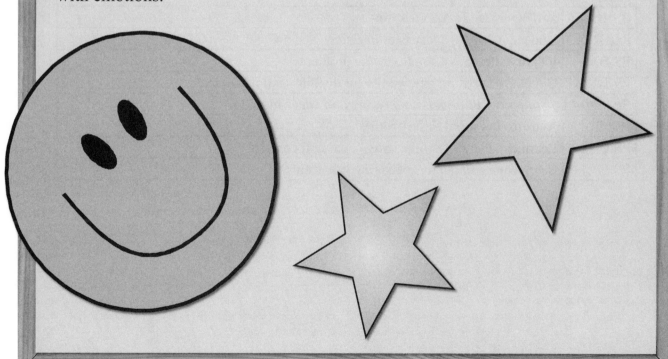

ASCA STANDARDS
FOR UNIT 8—FEELINGS

ACADEMIC DEVELOPMENT	
Standard A: Students will acquire the attitudes, knowledge and skills that contribute to effective learning in school and across the life span.	
A:A3	**Achieve School Success**
A:A3.1	Take responsibility for their actions

PERSONAL/SOCIAL DEVELOPMENT	
Standard A: Students will acquire the knowledge, attitudes and interpersonal skills to help them understand and respect self and others.	
PS:A1	**Acquire Self-Knowledge**
PS:A1.1	Develop positive attitudes toward self as a unique and worthy person
PS:A1.4	Understand change is a part of growth
PS:A1.5	Identify and express feelings
PS:A1.6	Distinguish between appropriate and inappropriate behavior
PS:A1.8	Understand the need for self-control and how to practice it
PS:A2	**Acquire Interpersonal Skills**
PS:A2.7	Know that communication involves speaking, listening and nonverbal behavior
Standard B: Students will make decisions, set goals and take necessary action to achieve goals.	
PS:B1	**Self-Knowledge Application**
PS:B1.2	Understand consequences of decisions and choices
PS:B1.3	Identify alternative solutions to a problem
PS:B1.4	Develop effective coping skills for dealing with problems
Standard C: Students will understand safety and survival skills.	
PS:C1	**Acquire Personal Safety Skills**
PS:C1.10	Learn techniques for managing stress and conflict
PS:C1.11	Learn coping skills for managing life events

COUNSELING ON THE WALL! © 2009 MAR∗CO PRODUCTS, INC. 1-800-448-2197

SAY "YES" TO HAPPINESS

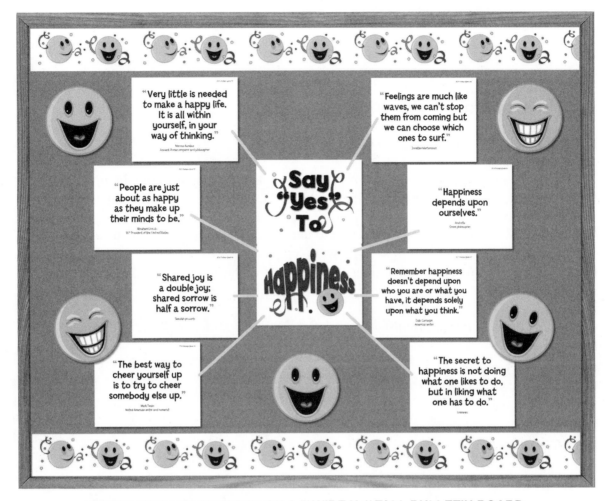

SAMPLE BOARD IS BASED ON A 5' WIDE X 4' TALL BULLETIN BOARD

Objective: To introduce students to coping skills for managing life events and encourage them to make good choices when dealing with emotions

Time: One 40-60 minute class period

Materials Needed:

For the leader:

☐ Green mural paper for the bulletin board background
☐ *Optional: Board 27 Smiley Faces Border* cut in half (included on CD)
☐ *Board 27 Title* (included on CD) or make the title from purchased bulletin board letters
☐ Selected *Board 27 Feelings Quotations* (included on CD)

- ☐ *Optional: Board 27 Large Smiley Faces* cut out (included on CD)
- ☐ White and/or colored paper for printing copies, preferably medium-weight
- ☐ Stapler and staples or glue
- ☐ Scissors
- ☐ *Optional:* Yarn

Pre-Presentation Preparation:

Cover the bulletin board with green mural paper.

Optional: Print enough copies of *Board 27 Smiley Faces Border* to frame the bulletin board. Cut the borders in half. Staple or glue the border to the bulletin board (see sample board).

Print *Board 27 Title*. Staple or glue the title to the bulletin board (see sample board).

Print the desired number of quotations. Staple or glue the quotations around the title (see sample board).

Optional: Print and cut out *Board 27 Large Smiley Faces* to decorate the board (see sample board).

Optional: Stretch yarn from the title to each quotation.

Directions:

Review the quotations with the students. Have them explain what each means and, if time permits, share examples from their personal experiences as they relate to the quotations.

COUNSELING ON THE WALL! © 2009 MAR∗CO PRODUCTS, INC. 1-800-448-2197

FEELINGS ARE LIKE WAVES...

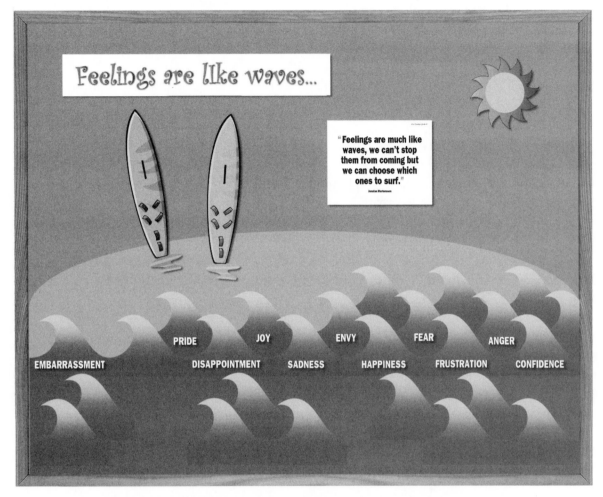

SAMPLE BOARD IS BASED ON A 5′ WIDE X 4′ TALL BULLETIN BOARD

Objective: To help the students understand that alternatives and choices can help them effectively deal with emotions

Time: One 40-60 minute class period

Materials Needed:

For the leader:

☐ Dark blue, light blue, and tan and mural paper for the bulletin board background

☐ *Board 28 Title* cut in half (included on CD) or make the title from purchased bulletin board letters

COUNSELING ON THE WALL! © 2009 MAR✳CO PRODUCTS, INC. 1-800-448-2197

- [ ] *Board 28 Feelings Quotation 5* (included on CD)
- [ ] *Board 28 Surfboards* cut out (included on CD)
- [ ] *Board 28 Sun* cut out (included on CD)
- [ ] *Board 28 Feeling Waves* cut out (included on CD)
- [ ] White and/or colored paper for printing copies, preferably medium-weight
- [ ] Stapler and staples or glue
- [ ] Scissors

Pre-Presentation Preparation:

Cover the top of the bulletin board with light blue mural paper. Cover the middle of the bulletin board with tan mural paper to create a beach. Cover the bottom of the bulletin board with darker blue mural paper to create an ocean. This looks best if the blue closely matches the dark blue of the waves (see sample board).

Print and cut in half *Board 28 Title*. Staple or glue the title to the bulletin board (see sample board).

Print *Board 28 Feelings Quotation 5*. Staple or glue the quotation to the bulletin board (see sample board).

Print and cut out *Board 28 Feeling Waves*. Staple or glue each wave to darker blue mural paper (see sample board).

Optional: Print and cut out *Board 28 Surfboards*. Staple or glue the surfboards to the bulletin board (see sample board).

Optional: Print and cut out *Board 28 Sun*. Staple or glue the sun to the bulletin board (see sample board).

Directions:

Select or have the students select a feeling and discuss situations in which it may occur. Students may personalize their contributions by telling about a time when they felt this feeling.

COUNSELING ON THE WALL! © 2009 MAR✶CO PRODUCTS, INC. 1-800-448-2197

WE ALL HAVE FEELINGS

SAMPLE BOARD IS BASED ON A 5' WIDE X 4' TALL BULLETIN BOARD

Objective: To teach students to identify and express their feelings

Time: One 40-60 minute class period

Materials Needed:

For the leader:

☐ Blue mural paper for the bulletin board background

☐ *Board 29 Title* (included on CD) or make the title from purchased bulletin board letters

☐ *Board 29 Comfortable Feelings Balloons* cut out (included on CD)

☐ *Board 29 Uncomfortable Feelings Balloons* cut out (included on CD)

☐ White and/or colored paper for printing copies, preferably medium-weight

☐ Stapler and staples or glue
☐ Scissors
☐ Yarn or string

Pre-Presentation Preparation:

Cover the bulletin board with blue mural paper.

Print *Board 29 Title*. Staple or glue the title to the bulletin board (see sample board).

Print and cut out *Board 29 Comfortable Feelings Balloons*. Staple or glue the balloons in a cluster on the bulletin board. Attach taut yarn or string from the balloons to the bottom of the board (see sample board). (*Note*: Feel free to write additional "comfortable" feeling words on the blank balloons.)

Print and cut out *Board 29 Uncomfortable Feelings Balloons*. Staple or glue the balloons with the uncomfortable feeling words to the bulletin board. Yarn or string attached to these balloons should hang loose, as if they were being released into the air (see sample board). (*Note*: Feel free to write additional "uncomfortable" feeling words on the blank balloons.)

Directions:

Explain that *feelings* come from *thoughts*. Ask how students might release uncomfortable thoughts. (Encourage students to share feelings by talking or writing about them, and/or expressing them through art and music.)

Ask how students can hold onto comfortable and nice feelings. (Encourage students to remind themselves about good and wonderful things.)

COUNSELING ON THE WALL! © 2009 MAR∗CO PRODUCTS, INC. 1-800-448-2197

Anger/Conflict Resolution

If not managed and controlled, anger can get a person into trouble! The counselor should strive to teach children to recognize this powerful emotion and take steps to calm themselves, such as by counting down from 10, breathing deeply, replacing angry thoughts with peaceful thoughts, talking calmly to themselves, and relaxing their muscles.

Once children learn to calm down, they can use problem-solving skills to handle problems that trigger anger. Students should consider the consequences of each option before making a decision about the best way to resolve a conflict.

This section's bulletin boards remind students to calm down, then try to work through the problem.

ASCA STANDARDS
FOR UNIT 9—
ANGER/CONFLICT RESOLUTION

ACADEMIC DEVELOPMENT	
Standard A: Students will acquire the attitudes, knowledge and skills that contribute to effective learning in school and across the life span.	
A:A3	**Achieve School Success**
A:A3.1	Take responsibility for their actions

PERSONAL/SOCIAL DEVELOPMENT	
Standard A: Students will acquire the knowledge, attitudes and interpersonal skills to help them understand and respect self and others.	
PS:A1	**Acquire Self-Knowledge**
PS:A1.1	Develop positive attitudes toward self as a unique and worthy person
PS:A1.4	Understand change is a part of growth
PS:A1.5	Identify and express feelings
PS:A1.6	Distinguish between appropriate and inappropriate behavior
PS:A1.8	Understand the need for self-control and how to practice it
Standard B: Students will make decisions, set goals and take necessary action to achieve goals.	
PS:B1	**Self-Knowledge Application**
PS:B1.2	Understand consequences of decisions and choices
PS:B1.3	Identify alternative solutions to a problem
PS:B1.4	Develop effective coping skills for dealing with problems
Standard C: Students will understand safety and survival skills.	
PS:C1	**Acquire Personal Safety Skills**
PS:C1.10	Learn techniques for managing stress and conflict
PS:C1.11	Learn coping skills for managing life events

COUNSELING ON THE WALL! © 2009 MAR★CO PRODUCTS, INC. 1-800-448-2197

FIND PEACE IN THE WORLD

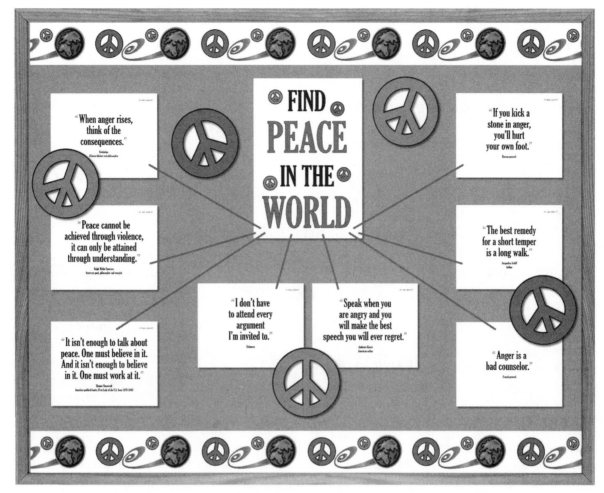

SAMPLE BOARD IS BASED ON A 5′ WIDE X 4′ TALL BULLETIN BOARD

Objective: To help students understand the need for self-control and anger-management

Time: One 40-60 minute class period

Materials Needed:

For the leader:

☐ Blue mural paper for the bulletin board background
☐ *Optional: Board 30 Earth Border* cut in half (included on CD)
☐ *Board 30 Title* (included on CD) or make the title from purchased bulletin board letters
☐ Selected *Board 30 Anger Quotations* (included on CD)

☐ *Optional: Board 30 Peace Signs* cut out (included on CD)
☐ White and/or colored paper for printing copies, preferably medium-weight
☐ Stapler and staples or glue
☐ Scissors
☐ *Optional:* Yarn

Pre-Presentation Preparation:

Cover the bulletin board with blue mural paper.

Optional: Print enough copies of *Board 30 Earth Border* to frame the bulletin board. Cut the borders in half. Staple or glue the border to the bulletin board (see sample board).

Print *Board 30 Title*. Staple or glue the title to the bulletin board (see sample board).

Print the desired number of quotations. Staple or glue the quotations around the title (see sample board).

Optional: Print and cut out *Board 30 Peace Signs* to decorate the board (see sample board).

Optional: Stretch yarn from the title to each quotation.

Directions:

Review the quotations with the students. Have them explain what each means and, if time permits, share personal examples that relate to the meanings of the quotations.

COUNSELING ON THE WALL! © 2009 MAR✶CO PRODUCTS, INC. 1-800-448-2197

1, 2, 3...PEACE BEGINS WITH ME

SAMPLE BOARD IS BASED ON A 5' WIDE X 4' TALL BULLETIN BOARD

Objective: To teach anger-management and conflict-resolution techniques

Time: One 40-60 minute class period

Materials Needed:

For the leader:

☐ Green mural paper for the bulletin board background

☐ *Board 31 Title* cut in half (included on CD) or make the title from purchased bulletin board letters

☐ *Board 31 Posters* (included on CD)

COUNSELING ON THE WALL! © 2009 MAR★CO PRODUCTS, INC. 1-800-448-2197

☐ *Optional: Board 31 Peace Sign* cut out (included on CD)
☐ White and/or colored paper for printing copies, preferably medium-weight
☐ Scissors
☐ Stapler and staples or glue

Pre-Presentation Preparation:

Cover the bulletin board with green mural paper.

Print and cut in half *Board 31 Title*. Staple or glue the title to the bulletin board (see sample board).

Print *Board 31 Posters*. Staple or glue the posters to the bulletin board (see sample board).

Optional: Print and cut out *Board 31 Peace Signs* to decorate the board (see sample board).

Directions:

Ask the students to describe some things people do that make them angry. (*Note:* Provide examples if the students cannot think of enough.) Using the examples and the steps written on the three panels of the bulletin board, students resolve the conflict.

COUNSELING ON THE WALL! © 2009 MAR∗CO PRODUCTS, INC. 1-800-448-2197

GET ON BOARD THE PEACE TRAIN

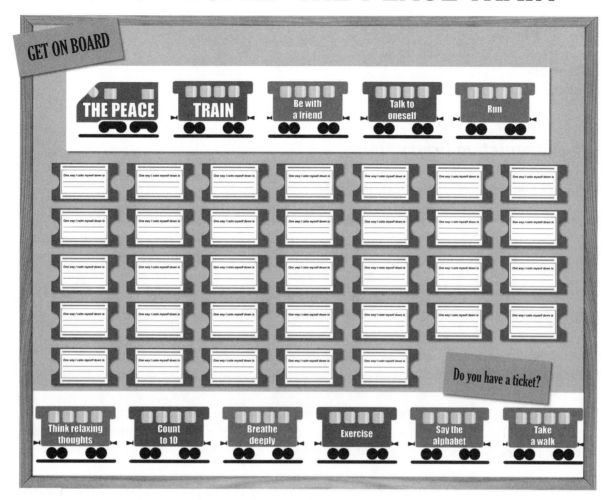

SAMPLE BOARD IS BASED ON A 5' WIDE X 4' TALL BULLETIN BOARD

Objective: To teach students techniques for managing anger and help them determine the methods that work best for them

Time: One 40-60 minute class period

Materials Needed:

For the leader:

☐ Gold mural paper for the bulletin board background

☐ *Board 32 Title* one page cut in half (included on CD) or make the title from purchased bulletin board letters

☐ *Board 32 Train Cars* (included on CD)

93

☐ White and/or colored paper for printing copies, preferably medium-weight
☐ Scissors

For each student:
☐ *Board 32 Ticket* (included on CD)
☐ Scissors
☐ Pencil

Pre-Presentation Preparation:

Cover the bulletin board with gold mural paper.

Print *Board 32 Title*. Staple or glue the title to the bulletin board (see sample board).

Print *Board 32 Train Cars*. Staple or glue the train cars to the bulletin board (see sample board).

Print and cut apart the *Board 32 Tickets*. Print one ticket for each student.

Directions:

When presenting a classroom lesson on anger management, explain that there are many ways to calm down. Tell the students what works for you. Discuss the calming techniques suggested on the train cars. Students suggest additional ways to calm themselves.

Emphasize the title *Get On Board The Peace Train*. Say that to get on the train, each student needs a ticket that identifies his/her best way to calm down.

Give each student a *Board 32 Ticket*, scissors, and a pencil. Students complete the sentence starter: *One way I calm myself down is* _____. Students cut out and sign their tickets.

Attach the completed tickets to the board.

On your next classroom visit, each student describes a time since the last visit that he/she got angry and used the calming technique written on his/her ticket.

COUNSELING ON THE WALL! © 2009 MAR∗CO PRODUCTS, INC. 1-800-448-2197

UNIT 10

Safety/ Drug Abuse Prevention

Elementary counselors encourage students to make thoughtful, healthy choices. Many topics in the guidance curriculum—including dealing with feelings, succeeding in school, making and keeping friends, steps to effective problem-solving, and decision-making skills—can help guide students to choose a drug-free life. "Think before you act" and "Consider the consequences" are familiar phrases in guidance lessons.

Red Ribbon Week, usually celebrated during the last week in October, is often a time when drug-free messages are promoted. The following bulletin boards help communicate *safety* and the drug-free message.

ASCA STANDARDS FOR UNIT 10— SAFETY/DRUG ABUSE PREVENTION

PERSONAL/SOCIAL DEVELOPMENT	
Standard A: Students will acquire the knowledge, attitudes and interpersonal skills to help them understand and respect self and others.	
PS:A1	**Acquire Self-Knowledge**
PS:A1.1	Develop positive attitudes toward self as a unique and worthy person
PS:A1.6	Distinguish between appropriate and inappropriate behavior
PS:A1.8	Understand the need for self-control and how to practice it
Standard B: Students will make decisions, set goals and take necessary action to achieve goals.	
PS:B1	**Self-Knowledge Application**
PS:B1.2	Understand consequences of decisions and choices
PS:B1.4	Develop effective coping skills for dealing with problems
Standard C: Students will understand safety and survival skills.	
PS:C1	**Acquire Personal Safety Skills**
PS:C1.11	Learn coping skills for managing life events

COUNSELING ON THE WALL! © 2009 MAR★CO PRODUCTS, INC. 1-800-448-2197

BE SAFE! THINK BEFORE YOU ACT!

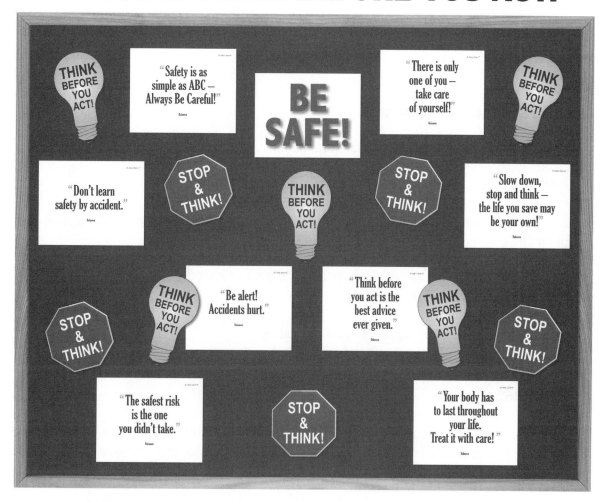

SAMPLE BOARD IS BASED ON A 5' WIDE X 4' TALL BULLETIN BOARD

Objective: To help students learn that they can use effective problem-solving and decision-making skills to make safe and healthy choices

Time: One 40-60 minute class period

Materials Needed:

For the leader:
- ☐ Dark blue mural paper for the bulletin board background
- ☐ *Board 33 Title* (included on CD) or make the title from purchased bulletin board letters
- ☐ Selected *Board 33 Safety Quotations* (included on CD)

- ☐ *Board 33 Stop Think* (included on CD)
- ☐ White and/or colored paper for printing copies, preferably medium-weight
- ☐ Stapler and staples or glue
- ☐ Scissors
- ☐ *Optional:* Yarn

Pre-Presentation Preparation:

Cover the bulletin board with dark blue mural paper.

Print *Board 33 Title*. Staple or glue the title to the bulletin board (see sample board).

Print the desired number of quotations. Staple or glue the quotations around the title (see sample board).

Optional: Print and cut out *Board 33 Stop Think*. Staple or glue the stop signs and light bulbs on the board (see sample board).

Optional: Stretch yarn from the title to each quotation.

Directions:

Divide the students into groups equal to the number of chosen quotations. Assign each group one quotation from the bulletin board. Students work together to come up with a 1-2 minute presentation explaining how the quotation relates to *safety* and *drug-abuse prevention.*

COUNSELING ON THE WALL! © 2009 MAR✳CO PRODUCTS, INC. 1-800-448-2197

RED RIBBON WEEK

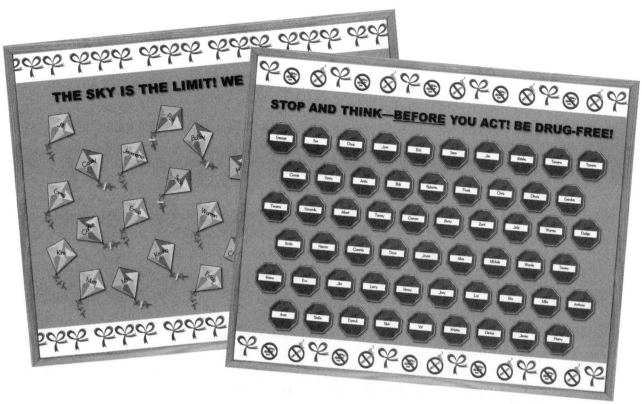

SAMPLE BOARDS ARE BASED ON A 5' WIDE X 4' TALL BULLETIN BOARD

15 Drug-Abuse Prevention Bulletin Boards For
Red Ribbon Week

Elementary counselors are often the leaders of schools' *Red Ribbon Week* celebrations. Usually observed during the last full week of October, *Red Ribbon Week* is the largest and oldest drug-prevention campaign in the United States. It's an ideal way for children to take a visible stand against drugs.

The following 15 bulletin board ideas support the drug-free cause.

Each bulletin board can be expanded to a participatory school-wide activity. If using the bulletin board titled *Put A Cap On Drugs*, for example, encourage students to wear their caps for an entire school day.

Objective: To help students learn about the emotional and physical dangers of substance use and abuse and encourage them to pledge to remain drug-free.

COUNSELING ON THE WALL! © 2009 MAR⋆CO PRODUCTS, INC. 1-800-448-2197

Time: One 40-60 minute class period

Pre-Presentation Preparation For The
Drug-Abuse Prevention Bulletin Boards:

- Cover the bulletin board with mural paper in any color.

- *Optional:* Print enough copies of the selected *Red Ribbon Border* or a border from another bulletin board unit to frame the bulletin board. Cut the borders in half. Staple or glue the border to the bulletin board.

- Make the title from purchased bulletin board letters. Staple or glue the title to the bulletin board.

- Print a copy of the *Shape* for each student or class. Have the students decorate, sign, and cut out the shapes to show support for a drug-free America.

Drug-Abuse Prevention Bulletin Boards:

BULLETIN BOARD #34:
TITLE: Our Future Looks Bright—We Are Drug Free!
Make the title from purchased bulletin board letters. Reproduce the *Board 34 Stars* (included on CD) on different-colored paper for every classroom in your school. Give each student in each classroom the same color star. After writing the name of his/her classroom on the star, the student cuts it out and signs it. Arrange the stars in a rainbow shape on the bulletin board or wall.

BULLETIN BOARD #35:
TITLE: We Pledge To Be Drug-Free
Make the title from purchased bulletin board letters. Reproduce a *Board 35 Hand Pledge* (included on CD) for each student in the school. Each student signs and cuts out his/her hand shape. Attach the hand shapes to the bulletin board or wall.

BULLETIN BOARD #36:
TITLE: The Sky Is The Limit! We Are Drug-Free!
Make the title from purchased bulletin board letters. Reproduce a *Board 36 Kite* (included on CD) for each student in the school. Each student decorates, signs, and cuts out his/her kite. Attach yarn or string to the end of each kite. Attach the kites to a bulletin board or wall.

COUNSELING ON THE WALL! © 2009 MAR✶CO PRODUCTS, INC. 1-800-448-2197

BULLETIN BOARD #37:
TITLE: Stop And Think—BEFORE You Act! Be Drug-Free!
Make the title from purchased bulletin board letters. Reproduce a *Board 37 Stop Sign* (included on CD) for each student. Each student signs and cuts out his/her stop sign. Attach the stop signs to the bulletin board or wall.

BULLETIN BOARD #38:
TITLE: We Are The Future, Let's Make It Drug-Free!
Make the title from purchased bulletin board letters. Reproduce a *Board 38 Space Ship* (included on CD) for each student. Each student decorates, signs, and cuts out his/her space ship. Attach the space ships to the bulletin board or wall.

BULLETIN BOARD #39:
TITLE: Put A Cap On Drugs!
Make the title from purchased bulletin board letters. Reproduce a *Board 39 Cap* (included on CD) for each student. Each student decorates, signs, and cuts out his/her cap. Attach the caps to the bulletin board or wall. If desired, put real caps on the board between the paper caps.

BULLETIN BOARD #40:
TITLE: Born To Be Drug-Free!

Make the title from purchased bulletin board letters. Ask the students to bring in baby pictures to put on the board. Or distribute *Board 40 Frames* (included on CD) and have each student draw a baby picture of him/herself, then cut out the frame. Attach the framed baby pictures or drawings to the bulletin board or wall.

BULLETIN BOARD #41:
TITLE: Drug-Free—The Way To Be!
Make the title from purchased bulletin board letters. Reproduce a *Board 41 Picture Frame* (included on CD) for each student. Have each student create a self-portrait with a HUGE smile on his/her face, then cut out the frame. Attach the framed drawings to the bulletin board or wall.

BULLETIN BOARD #42:
TITLE: Shoot For The Stars, Stay Drug-Free!
Make the title from purchased bulletin board letters. Cover the bulletin board with dark blue mural paper. Reproduce a *Board 42 Shooting Star* (included on CD) for each student. Each student decorates, signs, and cuts out his/her star. Attach the stars to the bulletin board.

COUNSELING ON THE WALL! © 2009 MAR✶CO PRODUCTS, INC. 1-800-448-2197

BULLETIN BOARD #43:

TITLE: Step Forward And Be Drug-Free!

Make the title from purchased bulletin board letters. Reproduce a *Board 43 Footprint* (included on CD) for each student. Each student decorates, signs, and cuts out his/her footprint. Attach the footprints to the bulletin board.

BULLETIN BOARD #44:

TITLE: Too Cool For Drugs!

Make the title from purchased bulletin board letters. Reproduce a *Board 44 Self-Portrait* (included on CD) for each student. Each students draws a self-portrait, signs, and cuts out his/her drawing. Attach the students' self-portraits to the bulletin board.

BULLETIN BOARD #45:

TITLE: Living Drug-Free Is No Sweat!

Make the title from purchased bulletin board letters. Reproduce a *Board 45 T-Shirt* (included on CD) for each student. Have the students design a "Drug-Free" Logo. Each student decorates, signs, and cuts out his/her T-shirt. Attach the T-shirts to the bulletin board.

BULLETIN BOARD #46:

TITLE: Team Up Against Drugs!

Make the title from purchased bulletin board letters. Reproduce a *Board 46 T-Shirt* (included on CD) for each student. Have the students decorate their shirts with their favorite sports team in mind. Each student signs and cuts out his/her T-shirt. Attach the T-shirts to the bulletin board.

BULLETIN BOARD #47:

TITLE: Sock It To Drugs!

Reproduce a *Board 47 Sock* (included on CD) for each student. Have each student design a unique pattern for his/her sock. Each student signs and cuts out his/her sock. Attach the completed socks to the bulletin board.

BULLETIN BOARD #48:

TITLE: United We Stand For A Drug Free Land!

Using red, white, and blue construction paper, reproduce a *Board 48 Paper Doll* (included on CD) for each student. Each student signs and cuts out his/her paper doll. Attach the paper dolls hand to hand to give the bulletin board a patriotic look.

COUNSELING ON THE WALL! © 2009 MAR*CO PRODUCTS, INC. 1-800-448-2197

UNIT 11

Character

The counselor often takes the lead in school character-education programs. Respect, responsibility, caring, cooperation, service, humanity, honesty, self-control, and good manners are just a few of the traits included under the wide umbrella called character education.

A good way to begin teaching character education is to let students know that good character is an important key to success in life. The following bulletin boards reinforce your character education program.

ASCA STANDARDS
FOR UNIT 11—CHARACTER

ACADEMIC DEVELOPMENT	
Standard A: Students will acquire the attitudes, knowledge and skills that contribute to effective learning in school and across the life span.	
A:A1	**Improve Academic Self-concept**
A:A1.5	Identify attitudes and behaviors that lead to successful learning
A:A3	**Achieve School Success**
A:A3.1	Take responsibility for their actions
Standard B: Students will complete school with the academic preparation essential to choose from a wide range of substantial post- secondary options, including college.	
A:B1	**Improve Learning**
A:B1.1	Demonstrate the motivation to achieve individual potential
A:B1.7	Become a self-directed and independent learner

CAREER DEVELOPMENT	
Standard A: Students will acquire the skills to investigate the world of work in relation to knowledge of self and to make informed career decisions.	
C:A1	**Develop Career Awareness**
C:A1.4	Learn how to interact and work cooperatively in teams
C:A1.5	Learn to make decisions
C:A1.6	Learn how to set goals

PERSONAL/SOCIAL DEVELOPMENT	
Standard A: Students will acquire the knowledge, attitudes and interpersonal skills to help them understand and respect self and others.	
PS:A1	**Acquire Self-Knowledge**
PS:A1.1	Develop positive attitudes toward self as a unique and worthy person
PS:A1.4	Understand change is a part of growth
PS:A1.6	Distinguish between appropriate and inappropriate behavior
PS:A1.8	Understand the need for self-control and how to practice it
PS:A1.10	Identify personal strengths and assets
PS:A2	**Acquire Interpersonal Skills**
PS:A2.1	Recognize that everyone has rights and responsibilities
PS:A2.2	Respect alternative points of view
PS:A2.3	Recognize, accept, respect and appreciate individual differences

COUNSELING ON THE WALL! © 2009 MAR✳CO PRODUCTS, INC. 1-800-448-2197

Standard B: Students will make decisions, set goals and take necessary action to achieve goals.	
PS:B1	**Self-Knowledge Application**
PS:B1.2	Understand consequences of decisions and choices
PS:B1.3	Identify alternative solutions to a problem

COUNSELING ON THE WALL! © 2009 MAR★CO PRODUCTS, INC. 1-800-448-2197

GOOD CHARACTER COUNTS

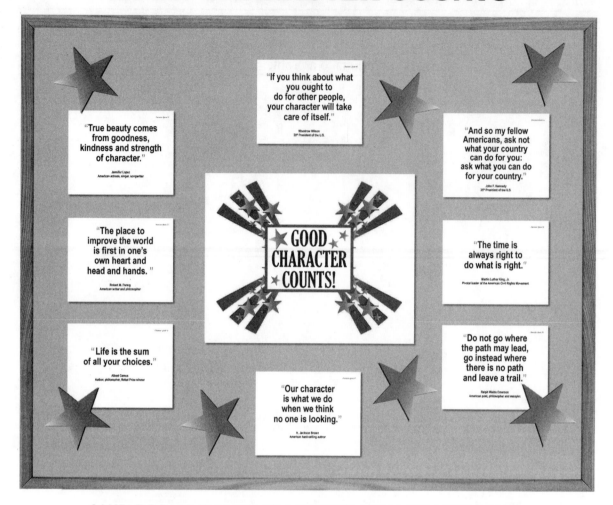

SAMPLE BOARD IS BASED ON A 5' WIDE X 4' TALL BULLETIN BOARD

Objective: To help students learn the importance of good character at school and in life

Time: One 40-60 minute class period

Materials Needed:

For the leader:

☐ Gold mural paper for the bulletin board background
☐ *Optional: Board 49 Title Frame* (included on CD)
☐ *Board 49 Title* (included on CD) or make the title from purchased bulletin board letters
☐ Selected *Board 49 Character Quotations* (included on CD)

COUNSELING ON THE WALL! © 2009 MAR★CO PRODUCTS, INC. 1-800-448-2197

- ☐ *Optional: Board 49 Blue Stars* (included on CD)
- ☐ White and/or colored paper for printing copies, preferably medium-weight
- ☐ Stapler and staples or glue
- ☐ Scissors
- ☐ *Optional:* Yarn

For each student:
- ☐ Drawing paper
- ☐ Crayons or markers

Pre-Presentation Preparation:

Cover the bulletin board with gold mural paper.

Optional: Print two copies of each page of the *Board 49 Title Frame*. Staple or glue the frame to the bulletin board (see sample board).

Print *Board 49 Title*. Staple or glue the title to the bulletin board (see sample board).

Print the desired number of quotations. Staple or glue the quotations around the title (see sample board).

Optional: Print and cut out *Board 49 Blue Stars* to decorate the board (see sample board).

Optional: Stretch yarn from the title to each quotation.

Directions:

Choose one or two quotations that you believe are most appropriate for your students' age and lead the students in a discussion about the meaning of the quotation(s). Give each student drawing paper and crayons or markers to draw a poster symbolizing the selected quotations.

COUNSELING ON THE WALL! © 2009 MAR∗CO PRODUCTS, INC. 1-800-448-2197

CHARACTER IS HEART, HEAD, AND HANDS

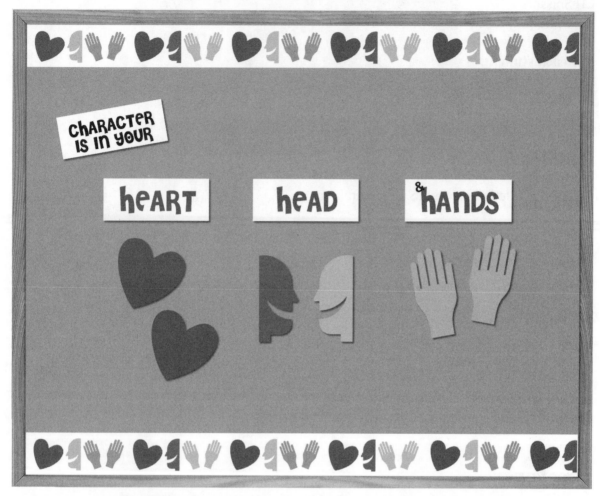

SAMPLE BOARD IS BASED ON A 5' WIDE X 4' TALL BULLETIN BOARD

Objective: To help students learn that good character is reflected in thoughts, words, and deeds

Time: One 40-60 minute class period

Materials Needed:

For the leader:

☐ Blue mural paper for the bulletin board background

☐ *Optional: Board 50 Head Hand Border* cut in half (included on CD)

COUNSELING ON THE WALL! © 2009 MAR★CO PRODUCTS, INC. 1-800-448-2197

- ☐ *Board 50 Title* cut in half (included on CD) or make the title from purchased bulletin board letters
- ☐ *Board 50 Heart* cut out (included on CD)
- ☐ *Board 50 Heads* cut out (included on CD)
- ☐ *Board 50 Hands* cut out (included on CD)
- ☐ White and/or colored paper for printing copies, preferably medium-weight
- ☐ Stapler and staples or glue
- ☐ Scissors

Pre-Presentation Preparation:

Cover the bulletin board with blue mural paper.

Optional: Print enough copies of *Board 50 Head Hand Border* to frame the bulletin board. Cut the borders in half. Staple or glue the border to the bulletin board (see sample board).

Print and cut in half *Board 50 Title*. Staple or glue the title to the bulletin board (see sample board).

Print and cut out two or more *Board 50 Hearts*. Staple or glue the hearts to the bulletin board (see sample board).

Print and cut out two or more *Board 50 Heads*. Staple or glue the heads to the bulletin board (see sample board).

Print and cut out two or more *Board 50 Hands*. Staple or glue the hands to the bulletin board (see sample board).

Directions:

Ask the students to name one thing in the world that needs improving and relate it to head, hands, and heart.

COUNSELING ON THE WALL! © 2009 MAR✱CO PRODUCTS, INC. 1-800-448-2197

GOOD CHARACTER
TAKES YOU TO THE TOP!

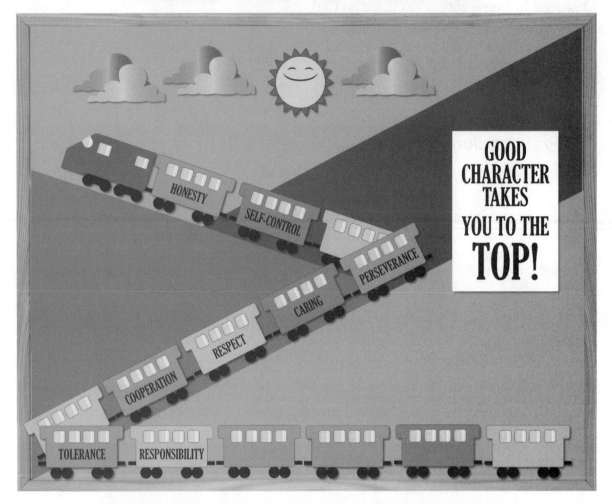

SAMPLE BOARD IS BASED ON A 5' WIDE X 4' TALL BULLETIN BOARD

Objective: To help students understand that good character will help them succeed in school

Time: One 40-60 minute class period

Materials Needed:

For the leader:

☐ Blue and shades of green or brown mural paper for the bulletin board background

☐ *Board 51 Title* (included on CD) or make the title from purchased bulletin board letters

COUNSELING ON THE WALL! © 2009 MAR★CO PRODUCTS, INC. 1-800-448-2197

- ☐ *Board 51 Train Cars* (included on CD)
- ☐ *Optional: Board 51 Clouds* (included on CD)
- ☐ *Optional: Board 51 Sun* (included on CD)
- ☐ White and/or colored paper for printing copies, preferably medium-weight
- ☐ Stapler and staples or glue
- ☐ Scissors

For each student:
- ☐ Drawing paper
- ☐ Crayons or markers

Pre-Presentation Preparation:

Cover the bulletin board with blue mural paper. Add green mural paper to create hills (see sample board).

Print *Board 51 Title*. Staple or glue the title to the bulletin board (see sample board).

Print and cut out *Board 51 Train Cars*. Staple or glue the train cars to the bulletin board (see sample board). (*Note:* Feel free to add your own character traits on blank train cars.)

Optional: Print and cut out several copies of *Board 51 Clouds*. Staple or glue the clouds to the bulletin board (see sample board).

Optional: Print and cut out *Board 51 Sun*. Staple or glue the suns to the bulletin board (see sample board).

Directions

After explaining the bulletin board, give each student drawing paper and crayons to draw an example of a how a trait written on the train is practiced in school.

COUNSELING ON THE WALL! © 2009 MAR✶CO PRODUCTS, INC. 1-800-448-2197

WHAT CAN YOU DO FOR YOUR COUNTRY?

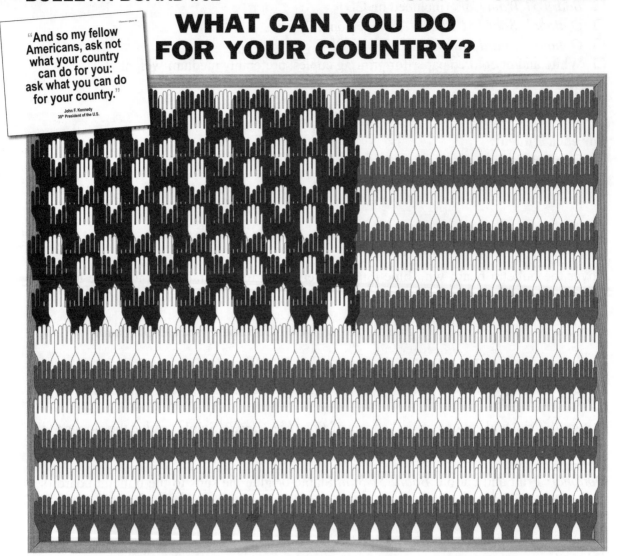

"And so my fellow Americans, ask not what your country can do for you: ask what you can do for your country."

John F. Kennedy
35th President of the U.S.

SAMPLE BOARD IS BASED ON A 5′ WIDE X 4′ TALL BULLETIN BOARD

(*Note:* This lesson is written for students in the United States of America. However, it can easily be adapted for children in other countries.)

Objective: To help students understand the importance of being good citizens of their country and the world

Time: One 40-60 minute class period

COUNSELING ON THE WALL! © 2009 MAR★CO PRODUCTS, INC. 1-800-448-2197

Materials Needed:

For the leader:
- ☐ White mural paper for the bulletin board background
- ☐ *Board 52 Character Quote 4* (included on CD) or make the title from purchased bulletin board letters
- ☐ White paper for printing copies, preferably medium-weight
- ☐ Stapler and staples or glue
- ☐ *Optional:* Board and chalk or chartpaper and marker

For each student:
- ☐ *Board 52 Red, White,* or *Blue Hand* (included on CD)
  or
  Red, white, or blue construction paper
- ☐ Black marker
- ☐ Scissors

Pre-Presentation Preparation:

Cut one red, white, or blue construction-paper rectangle large enough for each child to trace his/her hand. Or print, cut apart, and distribute one *Board 52 Red, White,* or *Blue Hand* to each student.

Print *Board 52 Character Quote 4.*

Directions:

This bulletin board works in conjunction with a classroom lesson on citizenship. Begin by explaining that having good character means being true to oneself and being a good citizen of one's country.

Share *Character Quote 4* with the students. Have the students brainstorm what they could do for their country. Say that you need their help to create a patriotic bulletin board.

Option 1:

Give each child a red, white, or blue construction-paper rectangle, marker, and scissors. (This takes a little planning. You'll need less blue paper than red or white. It's easiest to assign one color to each classroom.)

Each student traces his/her hand on the paper rectangle, writes his/her name on a finger and, on the palm, the act of citizenship he/she pledges to perform. Children too young to write may make the pledges orally, and you may write their names and pledges on the hands.

COUNSELING ON THE WALL! © 2009 MAR*CO PRODUCTS, INC. 1-800-448-2197

Option 2:

Give each child a *Board 52 Red, White,* or *Blue Hand Shape* and scissors. (This takes a little planning. You'll need less blue paper than red or white. It's easiest to assign one color to each classroom.)

Each student writes his/her name on a finger and, on the palm, the act of citizenship he/she pledges to perform. Children too young to write may make the pledges orally and you may write their names and pledges on the hands.

Staple or glue the cut-out handprints to the bulletin board.

To complete the assembly, attach *Character Quote 4* beneath or above the bulletin board. Use the students' hands to form the flag. (*Note:* In a very large school, you may want to make multiple bulletin boards and place them in different areas of the building, although a huge flag can be very impressive.)

Children share what they wrote on their hands. If desired, list the pledges on the board/chartpaper and discuss how these pledges could affect our country.

COUNSELING ON THE WALL! © 2009 MAR✶CO PRODUCTS, INC. 1-800-448-2197

Study And Test-Taking Skills

Elementary counselors are often their schools' "educational cheerleaders." In guidance lessons, counselors teach study skills and test-taking tips that help students succeed.

Study-skills lessons might include tips on how to stay organized, set effective goals, be a good listener, manage time, handle assignments responsibly, and the importance of proofreading. These skills should be taught in an age-appropriate manner each year.

Such test-taking hints as getting proper rest and eating a healthy breakfast, being prepared, having a positive attitude and taking time to read directions, proofreading, and effective study habits should also be included.

This section's bulletin boards reinforce the importance of good study habits and test-taking skills.

ASCA STANDARDS FOR UNIT 12— STUDY AND TEST-TAKING SKILLS

ACADEMIC DEVELOPMENT	
Standard A: Students will acquire the attitudes, knowledge and skills that contribute to effective learning in school and across the life span.	
A:A1	**Improve Academic Self-concept**
A:A1.5	Identify attitudes and behaviors that lead to successful learning
A:A2	**Acquire Skills for Improving Learning**
A:A2.4	Apply knowledge and learning styles to positively influence school performance
A:A3	**Achieve School Success**
A:A3.1	Take responsibility for their actions
Standard B: Students will complete school with the academic preparation essential to choose from a wide range of substantial post- secondary options, including college.	
A:B1	**Improve Learning**
A:B1.2	Learn and apply critical-thinking skills
A:B1.4	Seek information and support from faculty, staff, family and peers
A:B1.6	Use knowledge of learning styles to positively influence school performance
A:B1.7	Become a self-directed and independent learner
A:B2	**Plan To Achieve Goals**
A:B2.6	Understand the relationship between classroom performance and success in school
Standard C: Students will understand the relationship of academics to the world of work and to life at home and in the community.	
A:C1	**Relate School To Life Experiences**
A:C1.3	Understand the relationship between learning and work

PERSONAL/SOCIAL DEVELOPMENT	
Standard A: Students will acquire the knowledge, attitudes and interpersonal skills to help them understand and respect self and others.	
PS:A1	**Acquire Self-Knowledge**
PS:A1.1	Develop positive attitudes toward self as a unique and worthy person
PS:A1.3	Learn the goal-setting process
PS:A1.4	Understand change is a part of growth
PS:A1.10	Identify personal strengths and assets

COUNSELING ON THE WALL! © 2009 MAR∗CO PRODUCTS, INC. 1-800-448-2197

Standard B: Students will make decisions, set goals and take necessary action to achieve goals.	
PS:B1	**Self-Knowledge Application**
PS:B1.9	Identify long- and short-term goals
PS:B1.10	Identify alternative ways of achieving goals

COUNSELING ON THE WALL! © 2009 MAR✶CO PRODUCTS, INC. 1-800-448-2197

GET READY...GET SET...LEARN!

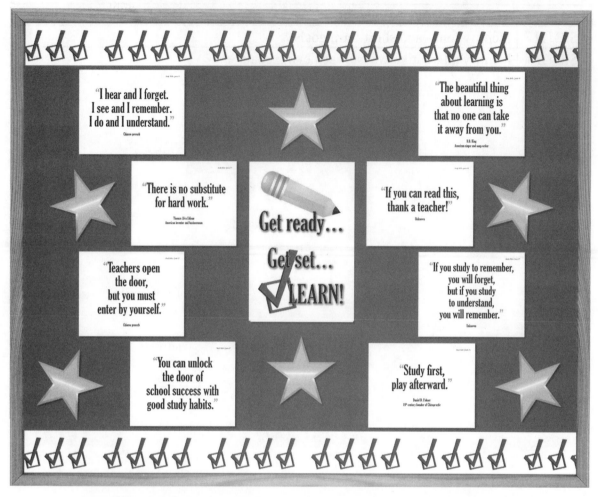

SAMPLE BOARD IS BASED ON A 5' WIDE X 4' TALL BULLETIN BOARD

Objective: To help students learn about attitudes and behaviors that can lead to successful learning

Time: One 40-60 minute class period

Materials Needed:

For the leader:
☐ Red mural paper for the bulletin board background
☐ *Optional: Board 53 Checkmark Border* cut in half (included on CD)
☐ *Board 53 Title* (included on CD) or make the title from purchased bulletin board letters

- ☐ Selected *Board 53 Study Skills Quotations* (included on CD)
- ☐ *Optional: Board 53 Gold Stars* cut out (included on CD)
- ☐ White and/or colored paper for printing copies, preferably medium-weight
- ☐ Stapler and staples or glue
- ☐ Scissors
- ☐ *Optional:* Yarn

Pre-Presentation Preparation:

Cover the bulletin board with red mural paper.

Optional: Print enough copies of *Board 53 Checkmark Border* to frame the bulletin board. Cut the borders in half. Staple or glue the border to the bulletin board (see sample board).

Print *Board 53 Title*. Staple or glue the title to the bulletin board (see sample board).

Print the desired number of quotations. Staple or glue the quotations around the title (see sample board).

Optional: Print and cut out *Board 53 Gold Stars* to decorate the board (see sample board).

Optional: Stretch yarn from the title to each quotation.

Directions:

Discuss each selected quotation with the students, having them relate its meaning to study skills.

COUNSELING ON THE WALL! © 2009 MAR★CO PRODUCTS, INC. 1-800-448-2197

DON'T PUZZLE OVER HOW TO TAKE TESTS

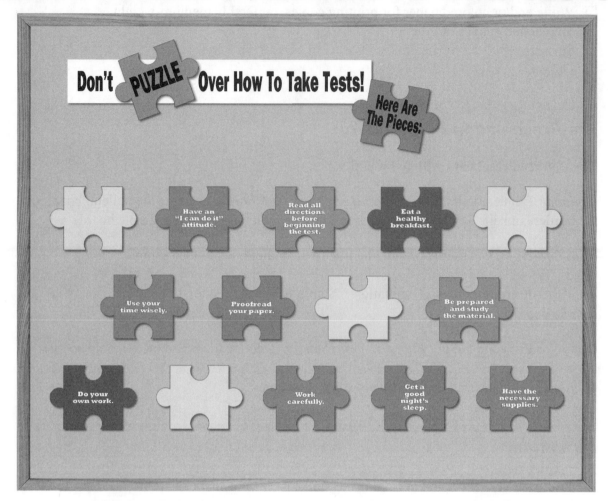

SAMPLE BOARD IS BASED ON A 5′ WIDE X 4′ TALL BULLETIN BOARD

Objective: : To help students identify habits that will improve their test-taking abilities

Time: One 40-60 minute class period

Materials Needed:

For the leader:
- ☐ Gold mural paper for the bulletin board background
- ☐ *Board 54 Title* cut in half/cut out (included on CD) or make the title from purchased bulletin board letters
- ☐ *Board 54 Puzzle Pieces* cut out (included on CD)

COUNSELING ON THE WALL! © 2009 MAR★CO PRODUCTS, INC. 1-800-448-2197

☐ White and/or colored paper for printing copies, preferably medium-weight
☐ Stapler and staples or glue
☐ Scissors

Pre-Presentation Preparation:

Cover the bulletin board with gold mural paper.

Print and cut out/apart *Board 54 Title*. Staple or glue the title to the bulletin board (see sample board).

Print and cut out *Board 54 Puzzle Pieces*. Staple or glue the puzzle pieces to the bulletin board (see sample board). (*Note*: Feel free to add your own study skills on blank puzzle pieces.)

Directions:

Assign different students a sentence starter relating to random study-skills suggestions at which you're pointing. For example: "You should proofread your paper because _____." or "It's important to do you own work because _____."

COUNSELING ON THE WALL! © 2009 MAR✶CO PRODUCTS, INC. 1-800-448-2197

YOU CAN UNLOCK THE DOOR
TO SCHOOL SUCCESS!

SAMPLE BOARD IS BASED ON A 5′ WIDE X 4′ TALL BULLETIN BOARD

Objective: To enable students to identify study skills necessary to succeed at each academic level

Time: One 40-60 minute class period

COUNSELING ON THE WALL! © 2009 MAR★CO PRODUCTS, INC. 1-800-448-2197

Materials Needed:

For the leader:
- ☐ Gold mural paper for the bulletin board background
- ☐ Brown or tan mural paper for the bulletin board door
- ☐ *Board 55 Title* (included on CD) or make the title from purchased bulletin board letters
- ☐ *Board 55 Success Keys* cut out (included on CD)
- ☐ *Board 55 Keyhole* cut out (included on CD)
- ☐ Gold and black construction paper for doorknob
- ☐ White and/or colored paper for printing copies, preferably medium-weight
- ☐ Stapler and staples or glue
- ☐ Scissors

Pre-Presentation Preparation:

Cover the bulletin board with gold mural paper.

Cover the center of the bulletin board with tan or brown mural paper to create a door (see sample board).

Make the door knob by cutting a rectangle from gold construction paper and a circle from black construction paper. Staple or glue the doorknob to the bulletin board (see sample board).

Print and cut out *Board 55 Keyhole*. Staple or glue the keyhole to the gold construction paper rectangle (see sample board).

Print *Board 55 Title*. Staple or glue the title to the bulletin board (see sample board).

Print and cut out (optional) *Board 55 Success Keys*. Staple or glue the keys to the bulletin board (see sample board). (*Note*: Feel free to add your own strategies for school success on the blank *Success Key*.)

Directions:

Divide the students into groups of two or three. Explain that every suggestion on the bulletin board is good, but that they may feel some are better than others. Tell them to imagine they may use only five of the suggestions and work together to choose the five they think are most important. Have each group share its findings.

COUNSELING ON THE WALL! © 2009 MAR✶CO PRODUCTS, INC. 1-800-448-2197

HOW I LEARN MY SPELLING WORDS

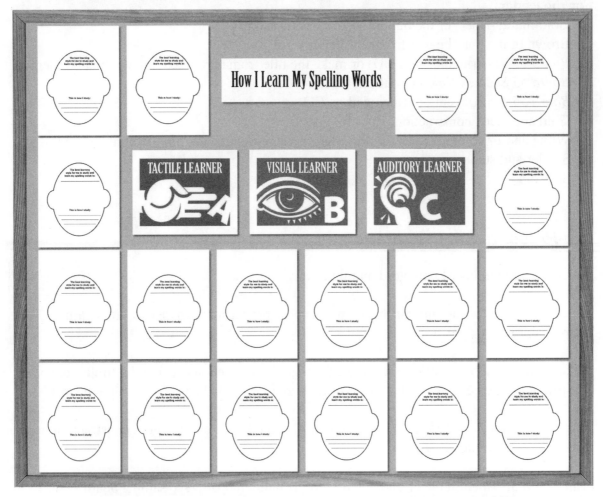

SAMPLE BOARD IS BASED ON A 5' WIDE X 4' TALL BULLETIN BOARD

Objective: To help students realize that identifying and using their distinct learning styles can positively influence school performance

Time: One 40-60 minute class period

Materials Needed:

For the leader:

☐ Gold mural paper for the bulletin board background

☐ *Board 56 Title* cut in half (included on CD) or make the title from purchased bulletin board letters

- ☐ *Board 56 Learning Styles* posters (included on CD)
- ☐ White and/or colored paper for printing copies, preferably medium-weight
- ☐ Stapler and staples or glue
- ☐ Scissors

For each student:
- ☐ *Board 56 Head* (included on CD)
- ☐ Pencil

Pre-Presentation Preparation:

Cover the bulletin board with gold mural paper.

Print *Board 56 Title*. Staple or glue the title to the bulletin board (see sample board).

Print *Board 56 Learning-Styles* posters. Staple or glue the three posters to the bulletin board (see sample board).

Print a *Board 56 Head* (with or without the sentence starter) for each student.

Directions:

This bulletin board may be presented during a classroom study-skills lesson. Explain that people learn in different ways. Someone who needs to hear information is an *auditory learner*. Someone who needs to see information is a *visual learner*. Someone who learns better when he/she moves around or touches information is a *kinesthetic* or *tactile learner*. Students give examples of how a visual, auditory, or kinesthetic learner might study spelling words. (*Note:* If students have difficulty giving examples, tell them an auditory learner could sing or say the words; a visual learner could look at the words carefully, break them into syllables, then study each part to find patterns; and a kinesthetic or tactile learner could write the words with his/her finger in a sandbox or jump rope while reciting the letters.)

Say that many people learn the best when they combine the three learning styles. Ask the students to brainstorm how they might combine all three methods. Example: A student could look at a word carefully, "write" the word with his/her finger, then sing the letters. Have each student decide how he/she learns best.

Give each student a *Head Shape* and a pencil to write about which learning style he/she uses to study spelling words each week. Ask any who say they don't study to write about which learning style would be good for them if they DID study the words. Have students use the

COUNSELING ON THE WALL! © 2009 MAR✱CO PRODUCTS, INC. 1-800-448-2197

sentence starter: "The best learning style for me to study and learn my spelling words is ___
_____. This is how I study:_____." Or have them write their ideas in the blank head
shape.

Have students sign their names and decorate the heads.

Attach the completed head shapes to the bulletin board.

Review the three learning styles. Divide the room into three parts. Each student moves to the
area that represents the learning style he/she uses most frequently. Tally the number of students
in each learning-style section, emphasizing that no style is better than any other.

COUNSELING ON THE WALL! © 2009 MAR✶CO PRODUCTS, INC. 1-800-448-2197

UNIT 13

Career Education

Students need to learn early that the education they are receiving in the present leads to success in the future. Though children do not need to choose their future career in elementary school, it is helpful to begin thinking of the world of work.

The counselor can begin career awareness activities as early as Kindergarten. These lessons will help students realize why each subject in school is important, why they need to make good educational choices along the way, and why becoming aware of their own strengths and weaknesses can lead to the job that is right for them as adults. The bulletin boards in this section can help reinforce the idea that school leads to future careers and choosing the right career path can result in happy, fulfilled lives.

ASCA STANDARDS
FOR UNIT 13—CAREER EDUCATION

ACADEMIC DEVELOPMENT	
Standard B: Students will complete school with the academic preparation essential to choose from a wide range of substantial post- secondary options, including college.	
A:B2	**Plan To Achieve Goals**
A:B2.6	Understand the relationship between classroom performance and success in school
Standard C: Students will understand the relationship of academics to the world of work and to life at home and in the community.	
A:C1	**Relate School To Life Experiences**
A:C1.3	Understand the relationship between learning and work
A:C1.5	Understand that school success is the preparation to make the transition from student to community member
A:C1.6	Understand how school success and academic achievement enhance future career and vocational opportunities

CAREER DEVELOPMENT	
Standard A: Students will acquire the skills to investigate the world of work in relation to knowledge of self and to make informed career decisions.	
C:A1	**Develop Career Awareness**
C:A1.2	Learn about the variety of traditional and nontraditional occupations
C:A1.7	Understand the importance of planning
Standard B: Students will employ strategies to achieve future career goals with success and satisfaction.	
C:B1	**Acquire Career Information**
C:B1.4	Know the various ways in which occupations can be classified
C:B1.8	Understand how changing economic and societal needs influence employment trends and future training
Standard C: Students will understand the relationship between personal qualities, education, training and the world of work.	
C:C1	**Acquire Knowledge to Achieve Career Goals**
C:C1.1	Understand the relationship between educational achievement and career success
C:C1.2	Explain how work can help to achieve personal success and satisfaction
C:C1.4	Understand that the changing workplace requires lifelong learning and acquiring new skills

COUNSELING ON THE WALL! © 2009 MAR∗CO PRODUCTS, INC. 1-800-448-2197

PERSONAL/SOCIAL DEVELOPMENT	
Standard A: Students will acquire the knowledge, attitudes and interpersonal skills to help them understand and respect self and others.	
PS:A1	**Acquire Self-Knowledge**
PS:A1.1	Develop positive attitudes toward self as a unique and worthy person
PS:A1.3	Learn the goal-setting process

COUNSELING ON THE WALL! © 2009 MAR✶CO PRODUCTS, INC. 1-800-448-2197

EDUCATION NOW = GOOD JOBS LATER!

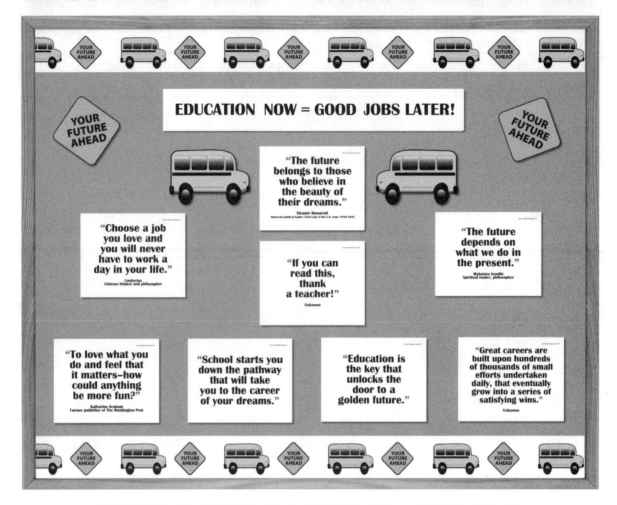

SAMPLE BOARD IS BASED ON A 5′ WIDE X 4′ TALL BULLETIN BOARD

Objective: To help students understand the relationship between educational achievement and career success

Time: One 40-60 minute class period

Materials Needed:

For the leader:

☐ Blue mural paper for the bulletin board background

☐ *Optional: Board 57 Bus Border* cut in half (included on CD)

130

- ☐ *Board 57 Title* cut in half (included on CD) or make the title from purchased bulletin board letters
- ☐ Selected *Board 57 Career Ed Quotations* (included on CD)
- ☐ *Optional: Board 57 Large Bus* cut out (included on CD)
- ☐ *Optional: Board 57 Future Sign* cut out (included on CD)
- ☐ White and/or colored paper for printing copies, preferably medium-weight
- ☐ Stapler and staples or glue
- ☐ Scissors
- ☐ *Optional:* Yarn

Pre-Presentation Preparation:

Cover the bulletin board with blue mural paper.

Optional: Print enough copies of *Board 57 Bus Border* to frame the bulletin board. Cut the borders in half. Staple or glue the border to the bulletin board (see sample board).

Print and cut in half *Board 57 Title*. Staple or glue the title to the bulletin board (see sample board).

Print the desired number of quotations. Staple or glue the quotations around the title (see sample board).

Optional: Print and cut out *Board 57 Large Bus* and *Board 57 Future Signs* to decorate the board (see sample board).

Optional: Stretch yarn from the title to each quotation.

Directions:

Students name careers that interest them. Select one or two quotations from the bulletin board and have the students relate their career choices to the meaning of the quotation(s).

COUNSELING ON THE WALL! © 2009 MAR✱CO PRODUCTS, INC. 1-800-448-2197

SCHOOL STARTS YOU DOWN THE PATHWAY

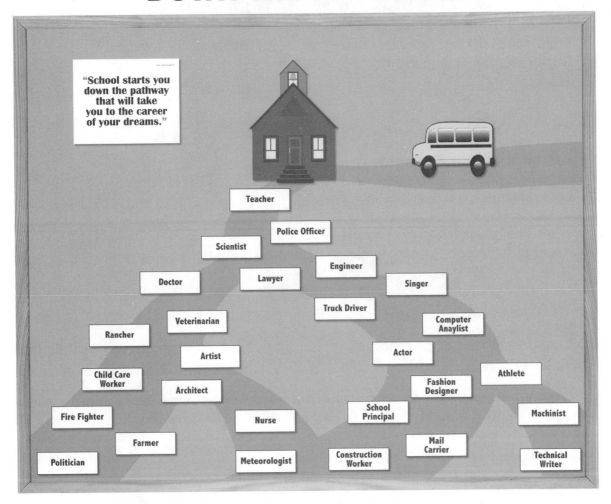

SAMPLE BOARD IS BASED ON A 5' WIDE X 4' TALL BULLETIN BOARD

Objective: To help students understand the relationship between personal qualities, education, training, and the world of work

Time: One 40-60 minute class period

COUNSELING ON THE WALL! © 2009 MAR✶CO PRODUCTS, INC. 1-800-448-2197

Materials Needed:

For the leader:
- [ ] Blue mural paper for the bulletin board background
- [ ] Gray or tan mural paper for the pathways
- [ ] *Board 58 Career Quote 7* (included on CD)
- [ ] *Board 58 School* cut out (included on CD)
- [ ] *Board 58 Career Cards* cut apart (included on CD)
- [ ] *Optional: Board 58 Bus* cut out (included on CD)
- [ ] White and/or colored paper for printing copies, preferably medium-weight
- [ ] Stapler and staples or glue
- [ ] Scissors

Pre-Presentation Preparation:

Cover the bulletin board with blue mural paper.

Use gray or tan mural paper to create paths from the school house (see sample board).

Print *Board 58 Career Quote 7*. Staple or glue the quote to the bulletin board (see sample board).

Print and cut out *Board 58 School*. Staple or glue the schoolhouse to the bulletin board (see sample board).

Print and cut apart *Board 58 Career Cards*. Staple or glue the cards to the paths on the bulletin board (see sample board).

Optional: Print and cut out *Board 58 Bus* to decorate the board (see sample board).

Directions:

Review the careers on the *Career Cards*. Students think of five careers they might like to explore. Tally their choices and, if desired, create a graph to show the number of students who chose each career. Or have the students rank their chosen careers from first to last.

COUNSELING ON THE WALL! © 2009 MAR✶CO PRODUCTS, INC. 1-800-448-2197

CHOOSE A JOB YOU LOVE

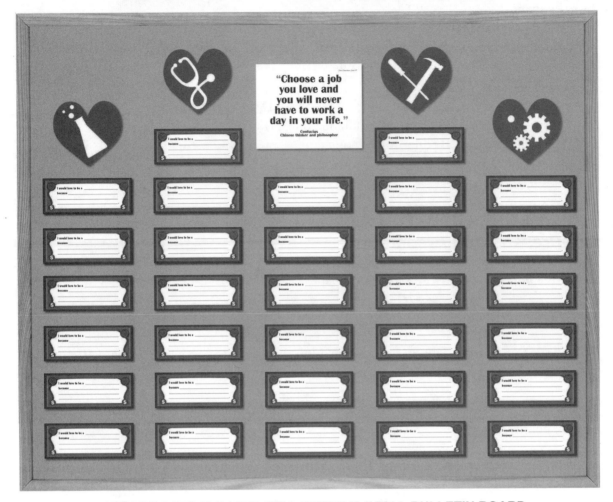

SAMPLE BOARD IS BASED ON A 5' WIDE X 4' TALL BULLETIN BOARD

Objective: To help students investigate the world of work in relation to self-knowledge needed to make informed career decisions

Time: One 40-60 minute class period

Materials Needed:

For the leader:

☐ Green mural paper for the bulletin board background

☐ *Board 59 Career Quote 3* (included on CD)

☐ *Optional: Board 59 Career Hearts* cut out (included on CD)

COUNSELING ON THE WALL! © 2009 MAR★CO PRODUCTS, INC. 1-800-448-2197

☐ White and/or colored paper for printing copies, preferably medium-weight
☐ Stapler and staples or glue
☐ Scissors

For each student:
☐ *Board 59 Career Dollar* (included on CD)
☐ Pencil
☐ *Optional:* Scissors

Pre-Presentation Preparation:

Cover the bulletin board with green mural paper.

Print *Board 59 Career Quote 3*. Staple or glue the quote to the bulletin board (see sample board).

Print a *Board 59 Career Dollar* for each student.

Optional: Print and cut out the *Board 59 Career Hearts* to decorate the board (see sample board).

Directions:

Begin the classroom career-awareness lesson by making sure the students understand why people work—for money, for personal satisfaction, and for enjoyment—if they're wise enough to choose a job that suits their talents and interests. Tell the students that Confucius, a wise Chinese thinker who lived centuries ago, spoke on this topic.

Share *Career Quote 3* with the students. Tell the students that even though they have a long time to think about what kind of job will make them happy, you'd like them say what job they'd choose if they had to decide today.

Ask what the quotation means. Discuss how to choose a career that will not seem like work.

Distribute *Board 59 Career Dollars*; pencils; and, if the students will be cutting out the dollar, scissors. Using the sentence starter: "I would love to be a _____ because _____ _____," have each student write about a job he/she would like to have. Or have the students put their names on the paper and write their ideas in the blank *Career Dollar*.

Attach the students' completed *Career Dollars* to the bulletin board.

COUNSELING ON THE WALL! © 2009 MAR✶CO PRODUCTS, INC. 1-800-448-2197

Mini Posters For The Guidance Office

When providing individual or group counseling in the guidance office, having posters on hand can be helpful. The following posters include prompts with feeling words, which can reinforce problem-solving and communication skills.

Got A Problem?
Work It Out!

State the problem fairly—without blaming other people

Brainstorm options to resolve the problem

Evaluate each option

What might happen?

Choose the best option

DO IT!

Did it work?
If not, what could you try next?

138

COUNSELING ON THE WALL! © 2009 MAR★CO PRODUCTS, INC. 1-800-448-2197

If You Want
A Friend,
You Must
<u>BE</u> A Friend!

- Make eye contact
- Smile
- Listen
- Ask others to play
- Help others
- Share

- Find out what others would like to do
- Take turns
- Play fair
- Think about others' feelings

COUNSELING ON THE WALL! © 2009 MAR★CO PRODUCTS, INC. 1-800-448-2197

FEELINGS:

We All
Have Them!

How Do You
Feel Today?

COUNSELING ON THE WALL! © 2009 MAR*CO PRODUCTS, INC. 1-800-448-2197

Sharing Your Feelings Is An Important Life Skill!

Don't Bottle Everything Up Inside...

Talk

Write

Express your feelings through art and music

Take positive action to find the way that is best for you!

COUNSELING ON THE WALL! © 2009 MAR∗CO PRODUCTS, INC. 1-800-448-2197

How To Deal With Bullies

▶ Report dangerous threats and situations
▶ Avoid bullies
▶ Ignore bullies
▶ Keep your sense of humor
▶ Act assertively around bullies
▶ Remind yourself that you don't have to believe the bully's message
▶ Stay with friends and stick up for one another other
▶ Talk to your counselor, your parents and teachers about problems you are having with bullies for other solutions
▶ Believe in yourself!

COUNSELING ON THE WALL! © 2009 MAR✳CO PRODUCTS, INC. 1-800-448-2197

ATTITUDE
IS EVERYTHING!

Keep going!

Fantastic!

I know I can attain my dreams!

I WILL succeed!

I can do it!

I am unique!

Brilliant!

Nothing can stop me!

WOW!

What a star!

I believe I can do it!

I am on the right track!

I am a winner!

I have many strengths!

My future is bright!

This year will be my best!

COUNSELING ON THE WALL! © 2009 MAR✲CO PRODUCTS, INC. 1-800-448-2197

ABOUT THE AUTHOR

Rosanne Sheritz Sartori was a classroom teacher and elementary counselor for 30 years. Toward the end of her career as an educator, she began her career as an author of guidance material. Her first two books, *Lively Lessons for Classroom Sessions* and *More Lively Lessons for Classroom Sessions,* are used by educators throughout the world.

Rosanne lives with her husband, Glenn, in St. Louis, Missouri and is constantly busy. Besides writing, she presents her ideas at schools and educational conferences, does volunteer work, makes jewelry, teaches art, and lives each day to the fullest. She believes that *enthusiasm* is the key to a full life.

Books By Rosanne Sheritz Sartori
Published By Mar*co Products, Inc.

A School of Champions!
Colorful Counseling! (Co-authored with Rachel Hood Herrman)
Lively Lessons for Classroom Sessions
More Lively Lessons for Classroom Sessions
Stand Up Against Bullies for Grades K-2
Stand Up Against Bullies for Grades 3-5